Draw On
YOUR RELATIONSHIPS

Second Edition

Draw on Your Relationships is a bestselling resource to help people of all ages express, communicate and deal more effectively with their emotions through drawing. Built around five key themes, each section contains a simple picture exercise with clear objectives, instructions and suggestions for development. The picture activities have been carefully designed to help ease the process of both talking about feelings and exploring life choices, by trying out alternatives safely on paper. This will help to create clarity and new perspectives as a step towards positive action.

Offering a broad range of exercises which can be adapted for any ability or age from middle childhood onwards, this unique book explores a range of emotions surrounding a person's important life experiences, key memories, relationships, best times, worst times and who they are as a person. This is an essential resource for therapists, educators, counsellors and anyone who engages other people in conversations that matter about their relationship to self, others and life in general.

This revised and updated second edition also contains a new section on how to use the superbly emotive *The Relationship Cards* (ISBN 9781138071018) to facilitate deeper therapeutic conversations.

Dr Margot Sunderland is Director of Education and Training at The Centre for Child Mental Health London, Senior Associate of the Royal College of Medicine and Child Psychotherapist with over thirty years' experience of working with children and families. Dr Sunderland is the author of over twenty books in child mental health, which collectively have been translated into eighteen languages and published in twenty-four countries. Her books, which form the *Helping Children with Feelings* series, are used as key therapeutic tools by child professionals all over the UK and abroad.

Nicky Armstrong holds an MA from the Slade School of Fine Art and a BA Hons in Theatre Design from the University of Central England. She is the principal artist at The London Art House and has illustrated over twenty books, which have been published in many countries. Nicky has also achieved major commissions nationally and internationally in mural work and fine art.

Draw On
YOUR RELATIONSHIPS

Second Edition

MARGOT SUNDERLAND
ILLUSTRATED BY NICKY ARMSTRONG

Routledge
Taylor & Francis Group
LONDON AND NEW YORK

Second edition published 2019
by Routledge
2 Park Square, Milton Park, Abingdon, Oxon, OX14 4RN

and by Routledge
711 Third Avenue, New York, NY 10017

Routledge is an imprint of the Taylor & Francis Group, an informa business

First edition published by Speechmark 2008

British Library Cataloguing-in-Publication Data
A catalogue record for this book is available from the British Library

Library of Congress Cataloging-in-Publication Data
A catalog record for this book has been requested

ISBN: 978-1-138-07070-7 (pbk)
ISBN: 978-1-315-11495-8 (ebk)

Typeset in Helvetica Neue Condensed
by Apex CoVantage, LLC
Printed by Ashford Colour Press Ltd

CONTENTS

INTRODUCTION

■About the book

We can only truly develop ourselves through our interactions with other people, and yet many children, teenagers and adults never sit down to reflect on their relationships. As a result, they may spoil their lives through repeating destructive relationship patterns, choosing people who are bad for them, staying in deadening relationships, or destroying the lovely relationships they *do* have.

This book is designed therefore to empower people to improve their quality of life by improving their relationships. It's a key resource for any professional whose work involves helping people to explore, communicate and learn more about themselves and their relationships. The photocopiable resources provide a creative and thought-provoking arena for people to stand back and reflect on their lives so that they can think, feel and act in more fulfilling and potent ways. The book provides step-by-step guidance on how to use the exercises with participants and how to develop a theme when the drawings have opened up a rich channel of communication.

■Underlying psychological insights backed by the latest research

In addition to the wealth of practical draw-your-feelings exercises, each section in the book offers the user key theoretical insights, backed by psychological or brain science research. These can then be passed on to the participant as appropriate. Furthermore, many of the frameworks for the exercises themselves are taken from in-depth psychotherapeutic concepts, which have been purposefully made palatable and accessible for anyone.

■Who the book is for

Many of the exercises are relevant for all age groups, except children younger than nine. Where an exercise has a specific client group or age range, this is clearly stated. Many sections of the book will be an excellent resource for the PSHE curriculum (personal, social and health education). The exercises are also designed so that participants can work at a depth of dialogue that feels comfortable. Moreover, whilst many of the exercises are appropriate for one person to do on their own, others are designed for two or more people to do together. These will be of particular value for times when the person leading the exercise, who I will call 'the practitioner', is working with a parent and child together, a couple, two work colleagues, a group or a family, or anyone else who undertakes the exercises, who I will refer to as 'the participant'.

How to use this book

This book is not designed to be worked through from cover to cover. Rather, the practitioner is encouraged to use the resource as follows:

1 Think about the child, young person or adult with whom you are working in terms of the relationship issues relevant to them. Then turn to the Contents page and select the most relevant section or sections. If, for example, people are struggling to trust in their relationships, you may decide to focus on 'Relationships and fear'. If they are spoiling their relationships by repeatedly getting locked into power and control issues, you may decide to work with 'Relationships and power'.

2 Turn to your chosen section and then read the few pages of theory at the beginning of the section. These are packed with easy-to-understand, evidence-based psychological concepts and will provide you with a vital understanding of why the person with whom you are working may be experiencing themselves, other people and life in general in the way that they are. The theory will also give you a firmer foundation from which to help your participant with their particular relationship or emotional issues.

3 Now turn to the exercises within your chosen section and read them through. Pick one or more that may be particularly relevant to the participant.

4 Familiarise yourself with the exercise and the 'Instructions' section. This section offers suggestions as to how you might *explain* the task to your participant. This section is not intended to be used in full, unless you wish to do so. In other words, the instructions should not be read out to your participant. Simply put them in your own words. Then photocopy your chosen exercises so that they are ready for your time together.

5 The 'Development' section offers another angle on the relationship issue, or another way of exploring the matter. It is obviously only relevant to use the tasks offered in these sections if your participant has been fully engaged in the exercise itself and clearly has more emotional energy around the theme. Remember, change can only happen if someone is emotionally engaged! The 'Development' sections and some of the exercises themselves refer to the use of sandplay. If you are unfamiliar with this excellent mode of expression and exploration, turn to the section called 'About sandplay and how to use it'.

6 The overall idea is to use the exercises to open up a rich and meaningful dialogue with the participant. When this happens, you may find that you have all manner of other creative ideas on how to develop a theme, rather than using the developments offered in the book. Allow your creative juices to flow! Only you know the particular needs of the person with whom you are working. So don't be afraid to offer developments that follow the participant along their own rich vein of ideas and feelings.

■Why work through feelings about relationships?

Why should it make such an enormous difference to communicate something to another person?

(Fosha, 2000)

Working through painful feelings means both feeling and reflecting on them in the presence of someone who, by adopting an empathic stance, can help you to feel and reflect. It is their very presence that makes it safe enough for you to do this. This 'active listener' engages in the process of imagining what it must feel like to be you, when you are feeling this way. Most importantly, they then find the right words to communicate that empathy. This means a profound, often deeply moving conversation, expressed so well in this passage by Dinah Craik in 1859:

Oh, the comfort, the inexpressible comfort, of feeling safe with a person; having neither to weigh thoughts nor measure words, but to pour them all out just as they are, chaff and grain together, knowing that a faithful hand will take and sift them, keep what is worth keeping, and then, with the breath of kindness, blow the rest away.

The result of working through feelings about painful relationship experiences is that the feelings can be modified, laid to rest, assimilated. In contrast, when feelings are not worked through they can continue to spoil and disrupt a person's life for days, months, years and sometimes for an entire lifetime. A woman lost a relative in a car crash and because she didn't go for help to work through the shock, whenever she heard a car horn, she had a panic attack. It was affecting her sleeping, eating, work and relationships. People say, 'The past is past'. This is exactly what it isn't. The past can't go into the past until it is worked through in the present.

So simply managing feelings about the people in your life, as opposed to working them through, can result in all manner of ongoing emotional and physical pain. It can even kill you. Here are two examples. When Sarah was 24, her little girl died of cancer. She said, 'When my angel died, the only way I could get through it was the drink'. At 26 Sarah was dead from alcohol abuse. After Simon lost his natural mother at age three and then was ripped away from his beloved foster mother at age eight, no one helped him to work through his feelings, so at age thirteen, he started to manage them by smoking. He died aged 42, from lung cancer.

We all manage emotional pain; we have absolutely no choice but to manage it. However, for many people their chosen method of managing can make them feel a lot worse. This is in direct contrast to 'working through', which results in heightened self-awareness, psychological strength and personal development. It also robs trauma and loss of their destructive impact on a person's life.

Why use drawings and images to speak about feelings?

When anyone asks, 'How are you feeling?' it is a huge transitional challenge to turn such subtle and dynamic neural processes into a verbal statement.

(Siegel, 1999)

The structured exercises in this book are designed to ease the process of working through relationship issues and to offer the participant a safe way to reflect on and reassess their relational world. The exercises offer a rich vocabulary for the participant to describe their experiences, and to engage their imagination as well as their thinking. As a result, it is hoped that the participant will see things more clearly and, where appropriate, move into creative action in their lives.

■But why not just speak about feelings using everyday language? Why use images?

Without images, people often use words that fail to fully capture what they want to say about a particular person or relationship in their life. They give an impoverished or over- generalised or inaccurate account of what they are feeling. This is very finely described by the famous Jungian analyst, James Hillman:

A person says, 'I feel depressed'. Now I don't know what that means. It's empty. No sensuous content, no image. The word . . . is a compromise with depression, which helps repress it, only admitting it in a vague, abstract way. So in practice I'll want to get precise, we are trying to get to the Venus language: the whole taste, body, image of the state of the soul in words. All that has disappeared and instead the big empty vapid jargon word, depression. That's a terrible impoverishment of the actual experience.

(Hillman, 1983)

Some people are emotionally literate and have a good inter-hemispheric communication between their right and left brain. We now know this is key to creativity (Aziz-Zadeh et al., 2012; Durante and Dunson, 2016). Nevertheless, they do not call on the full wisdom of the human brain's capacity for active use of imagery. They do not use drawings, art media or mental images to describe their experiences. The trouble is that if we just talk about relationship experiences and feelings in everyday language, it can often be predominantly the left brain speaking. This means a weaker truth, a smaller version of the deep feelings a person is experiencing. You can often tell if someone's left brain is dominant as their language for feelings is very dry, dull and devoid of image and metaphor. Their tone of voice is also often flat or colourless. In contrast, when the left and right brain are working together in a beautifully coordinated way through the coming together of thinking, feeling and imagining in use of drawing or other art media, there is often an incredible flow to the conversation, as eloquently expressed by Fosha:

[The process] is marked by effortless focus and concentration . . . imagery is vivid . . . the material flows. Relating is characterised by clear and effortless contact. The core state is one of deep openness – receptivity in which deep therapeutic work can take place . . . the atmosphere is highly charged, superficial interaction disappears, awareness is heightened and the work shimmers with meaning and importance . . . the sense of the experience coming, unbeckoned, rather than sought or willed: the intense sensations, including the upward surge . . . and the sensation of warmth . . . the sense of an even deeper state transformation.

(Fosha, 2000)

In short, we all have all the necessary software in our brains to enable us to successfully work through our painful life experiences and put down our emotional baggage once and for all. Tragically, many people never tap into this capacity.

■Key benefits from using the drawing exercises in this book to work through relationship issues

- The images can help people to 'see' what they cannot verbalise.
- The images call on the creative capacities of the participant to problem-solve their relationship issues rather than simply think about them.
- The images can support the process of communicating and exploring feelings in ways the person may not have done previously, simply because they did not have the means for doing so.
- The images can help free the participant from self-imposed limitations.
- With the help of the drawings as vital openers or triggers, people are often able to describe their perceptions and emotions far more exactly than with words alone.
- The exercises are an ordering process. Having completed them, many people experience a new clarity of thought.
- The exercises offer opportunities to rehearse healthier ways of relating to others, to try out more creative ways of thinking, feeling and relating, safely on paper.
- The exercises enable the participant to explore and express what they may have previously kept from others and often from themselves.

Image-making often comes very easily to people once they start, because it is actually very familiar to us. Much of our waking thought is in images and we create incredible images every night in our dreams.

How to work safely

Speaking about relationship issues through drawings is 'indirect expression'. This indirectness offers safety. The pictures in the exercises and those drawn by the participant are set apart from the self, seen from a standing-back position. In this way, they act as 'containers' for feelings which could otherwise be experienced as overwhelming, chaotic or unthinkable. Through the act of drawing or writing, the 'forming feeling' process is a way of creating external order out of inner chaos. Once the feelings are organised into an image on a piece of paper, they can be thought about in a clear, non-threatening way. This can bring real relief from having externalised what has previously been experienced only as raw, disturbing, unprocessed states. The sequence is as follows: *overwhelming feeling, through image, to thought-about feeling*.

Furthermore, because of the use of drawings, the actual relationship between practitioner and participant can be experienced as far less threatening than if feelings were being talked about without using any artistic modes of expression. There is literally something between the two people – the drawing; a focus outside of themselves. The drawings can also offer protection as described by Storr (1972): 'To show oneself only through . . . a picture . . . is to protect oneself, whilst at the same time enjoying the gratification of self-revelation'. In other words, safety comes from a sense of being once removed: 'I am not showing you me, I am showing you my drawing'.

■ 'What if I have no training in counselling or therapy?'

For people using this book who have no professional training in counselling or therapy, I reiterate the statement made on this matter in my book *Draw on Your Emotions* (Sunderland, 1993):

A lot of excellent informal untrained counselling goes on in the pub, over the garden fence, or in the school playground. If the relatively few people

trained as therapists or counsellors were the only ones 'allowed' to listen to the feelings of adults or children, there would be far more suffering and loneliness in the world than there is today.

That said, there are some key guidelines and structures for working safely with people's feelings on a more formal basis.

There will never be enough psychologists to address the massive human need for help with emotional and relationship issues. It is vital that far more people working with children, adolescents or adults are trained to work with *feelings* as well. Many excellent teachers, learning mentors, special educational needs coordinators (SENCOs), life coaches, social workers, probation officers, nurses and doctors find themselves managing a great deal of human distress, often on a daily basis. They need to be empowered to respond effectively and safely, so that far fewer people are left with no option but to turn to damaging forms of self-medication. Without more 'talking cure' interventions and skilled empathic listeners, we will continue to have the epidemic levels of mental ill health and debilitating long-term misery that we see today.

Key rules and guidelines in helping someone to speak about feelings

There are many natural 'therapists' whose warmth, empathy and compassion far outweigh that of people who have done years of formal training. That said, without clear guidelines and ground rules, an untrained or poorly trained practitioner can say something that they do not realise is hurtful, or even psychologically damaging. This is because when people talk about their feelings they let down their defences. They are then vulnerable and open to being really hurt.

By and large, damaging practitioner statements will be those that do one or more of the following: patronise, lecture, generalise, try to mind-read, misinterpret, infer meaning, offer platitudes, fail to acknowledge or validate the participant's experience of an event, criticise, accuse or assume what the participant is feeling when they aren't feeling it at all. If any of these things happen, the participants with a strong enough sense of self will manage to protect themselves by closing down, not talking about their feelings again, or not returning to the one-to-one sessions. Participants who don't know how to protect themselves, or who are out to please or comply, are far more vulnerable to suffering psychological damage from unskilled practitioners. Thus, for those people who are using the exercises in the book who have not undergone formal counselling or therapy training, we advise the closest observation of the following safety rules.

■1) Do not infer meaning

The danger many people fall into is playing 'psychoanalyst' by using closed meanings. For example, a snake means a penis, a sand mound means a breast, the drawing of a child between a man and a woman *always* means the person wants to split up mummy and daddy. Such interpretation is dangerous.

Although many outdated psychological and dream dictionaries try to define what a certain image means in this way, in reality what, say, a snake means to one person may be something entirely different to another. For one person a snake may mean a creature that is slowly plotting a sinister death; to another it may be like a large colourful worm with no frightening meaning whatsoever.

It is damaging for anyone to be told what they feel or think, when it is not what they are feeling and thinking at all. It can be experienced as a psychological assault, a violation, or an attempt to erase a person's own meaning, reality or sense of self. It is turning *their* experience into *your* experience. The awful thing is that some people will just put up with this abuse and think the professional must be right. They can start to lose a sense of who they are, and to see themselves as the practitioner sees them. Moreover, if you are repeatedly told what you are feeling, or what your images mean, it is actually mad-making. It is even worse than to be told that you are in denial if you disagree with the person who is dictating what you feel!

When emotionally healthy people who have a strong sense of self are treated in this way, the reaction is to back off and think: 'Well, here's someone who clearly can't listen to what I am feeling and just *tells* me what I am feeling. They are not curious to know what something means for them. They are certain what it means for me! It's not safe anymore to speak about my feelings to this person.' The emotionally healthy child will say something like 'Can we play football?' knowing they will never again bring feelings to this person. The trust is broken, and the practitioner is unlikely to win it back easily, if at all. A healthy adult or child will not return to a practitioner such as this. In contrast, the problem lies with the participant who just swallows unquestioningly the practitioner's *inaccurate* version of who they are, of what they are feeling and why they are feeling it. This participant often leaves the session feeling deeply disturbed, but without knowing why. It is this that can seriously damage mental health. Many people say, 'But I wouldn't interpret', and yet, unconsciously, they keep putting their own meanings on to the participant's drawings. Personal counselling, therapy and supervision for the practitioner can go a long way towards preventing this.

So always ask the participant what something means for them. You can say something like 'Will you help me to understand this?' or 'I wonder what that means for you?' If you don't understand the meaning of an image drawn by the participant, you can always interview the image.

Practitioner: It may be useful for us to learn more about the little flame in your picture. You said it was really important to you, but you didn't know why. I wonder if you would be prepared to enter more into the sense of this image, and for me to interview the flame?

(Participant agrees.)

So, little flame, tell me about yourself. How does it feel to be you? (Ask the participant to always start their reply with 'I' not 'it'. This engages the deeper-feeling right brain far more than the logical, rational left brain.)

Here are some possible questions when interviewing an image:

- What is life like for you, little flame?
- What do you need?
- What are you feeling at the moment?
- What frightens you?
- What pleases you?
- What are your innermost secrets?
- What are the best things about your life?
- What are the worst things?
- What do you want from life?
- How do you feel about your situation?
- How do you feel about being the size you are?
- What threatens you?

Each question can lead to further development. At the end of the interview, come in with an empathic summary.

Example

Practitioner: Hi little flame, what do you most need right now?
Participant: I need a safe shelter, otherwise I'll get blown out.

Practitioner (examples of where you could go next): So how might you get blown out? Who or what might blow you out? What would it feel like if you got blown out? What might happen then?
Participant: I am small and helpless, so a harsh uncaring wind could blow me out and then I fear I would no longer exist. There is no one there to help me.
Practitioner's summary: Wow little flame. You have told me such important things here, all about how unsafe things feel for you. How frightening to be you in this world when you feel there is no one to help you or protect you from a harsh wind.

■2) Check that your so-called observations are not actually incorrect interpretations

Example of an observation being an incorrect interpretation

Participant: When I am with this person in my life, I seem to go into a kind of cave. (The participant has given no indication of the feeling content of his image of the cave.)
Practitioner: Oh, how awful, it must feel terrible down there.

This is the practitioner's assumption. She herself might feel awful if she were in a cave. But in actuality, the cave might be a very comforting, safe place to the participant. So get more information from the participant by asking, for example, 'I'm wondering what it feels like for you in the cave', 'What sort of cave is it?'

Another example of a damaging interpretation

A child works in sandplay depicting what it is like for her to live with her alcoholic mother. She buries a little blue door in the sand, right at the bottom. One interpretative counsellor may think, 'This means the child feels swamped by her mother's alcoholism'. Another interpretative counsellor may think, 'Burying, this means that the child wants to hide from her mother's problem'. Such thoughts are all likely to be projections of what the counsellors themselves feel. For example, the first counsellor may be feeling swamped by something in her own life. The second counsellor may want to hide from something in her life or did so when she was a child. So simply ask the child, 'What is it like for the blue door being buried so far down?'

■3) Watch out for hidden incorrect assumptions in the choice of words you use in response to the participant's drawing or image

Example

Participant: When I am with my partner I feel like we are on a path in the middle of nowhere.

Practitioner: Where is the path leading? (The practitioner has brought in the concept of leading, not the participant. The path may not be leading anywhere!)

Or:

Practitioner: Tell me about that sad baby in your picture, looking out of the window. (The practitioner has brought in the concept of sad. Maybe she herself is feeling sad today. The baby may be just taking in the view. The participant has not given any indication that the baby is sad.)

Or:

Practitioner: Tell me about the drooping hat. (The adjective, 'drooping' is the practitioner's word. The hat may look droopy to her, but it may not be perceived as such by the participant, or if it is, it may be an irrelevant aspect of the hat.)

■4) Make sure you ask open, not closed, questions

What sort of questions to ask

Avoid at all times:

~~CLOSED QUESTIONS~~   ~~QUESTIONS NEEDING YES OR NO ANSWER~~

Ask open-ended questions, not questions that require a yes or a no. The latter are what are known as closed questions. So, instead of asking, 'Do you feel sad about it?' (closed question requiring a yes/no answer), ask, 'What do you feel about it?' (open-ended question).

For example, the participant says, 'I remember sitting alone in my room a lot as a child'. The practitioner asks: 'Do you feel angry about that?' This is a closed question, which requires a yes or no answer. The practitioner is imposing on the participant the concept of anger. In answering the question about anger, the participant will have to move out of her particular feeling and imagining and move into her left brain to consider whether or not she is angry. Such unfortunate interventions are often the result of the practitioner unintentionally projecting his or her own feelings on to the participant (maybe the practitioner is feeling angry today). The practitioner should have said something like, 'I wonder what you felt sitting there?' (open-ended question).

~~WHY~~

Never ask 'Why?' questions. 'Why?' again means that the participant must move away from their feelings into the logical, thinking and assessing part of their brain. And she may not know why. Sometimes it just is!

■5) Know how to work with half-said statements and unfinished sentences

The key to enabling someone to work through feelings is to help them to develop an idea or a theme, to stay with it, so that it can be fully explored, rather than to skate on the surface. So often people need help to get to and then stay with a point of awareness or insight. They may, for example, start a sentence but then leave it unfinished. Here is an example of a common situation, where it is vital for the practitioner to support the participant in staying with a feeling in order to work it through.

Participant: I feel fed up about this . . .
(It could have stopped there, but the practitioner follows on.)
Practitioner: You feel fed up about it because?
Participant: Because I am always letting myself down.

The participant still needs encouragement to stay, explore and deepen.

Practitioner: And that makes you feel?
Participant: Like smashing the whole world up.
Practitioner: Will you draw a picture of that?

After the participant has drawn a picture of major destruction and devastation, she is no longer feeling defeated but has moved into a strong place of protest.

Participant: I am not going to keep cheating myself in this way.

Within the next three months, the participant had harnessed all the energy she drew in her picture, changed her job, left her bullying boss and found a man who she was really starting to love.

The same ways of developing and deepening can be used with children. However, they may need the safety of staying in the metaphor. (For more on this, see Sunderland, 2002.)

■6) The importance for practitioners to process and work through their own emotional pain, trauma and loss

So much depends on the practitioner's own level of self-awareness if they are to offer the richest possible connection with participants, and to empower them to live a life characterised by emotional well-being and deeply satisfying relationships. This is why registered counsellors and therapists are all required to undergo their own in-depth counselling or therapy. When a practitioner has not worked through their own emotional issues, they can be blind to those in the people with whom they work. This means they may not be able to hear some forms of emotional pain. They may block the participant's expression or unintentionally invite a 'stiff upper lip' attitude. This is likely to strengthen the participant's defences, making him or her feel psychologically unsafe.

If the practitioner's inner world is emotionally impoverished or persecutory in some way, she may unwittingly squash the participant's vitality by flat responses and arid forms of relating. She may leave unborn aspects of enlivened humanness, which have thus far been un-evoked in the participant, and thus remain so. Moreover, the participant may internalise something emotionally deadened in the practitioner or something perhaps unwittingly shaming. This is very concerning, particularly for children who are often so open and undefended and therefore vulnerable to the blighting emotional energies of significant adults.

■7) Working safely and ethically with children and young people

Any professional who is helping children to work through feelings must undergo training in child protection and be fully aware of all the legislation specific to the welfare of children. Children can make a disclosure and it is vital that practitioners know what to do and who to refer to. I would also strongly advise that any practitioner working in schools read *Good Practice Guidance for Counselling in Schools* (McGinnis and Jenkins, 2006).

■8) Make sure you leave enough time at the end of a session to assimilate, summarise and reflect

Effective 'talking about feelings' sessions have a particular flow and rhythm about them. There is an opening time to re-establish a good connection and make sure you both have a good working alliance. Then there is a time of co-exploration of the key emotional themes you will address, using the drawings and developments as appropriate. At the end of the session, the practitioner needs to bring together all the significant and important strands of the session in a summary. For children it can be very effective to do this by doing a big drawing on a large A1 piece of paper. Draw and talk your summary at the same time, and then ask the child if you have got everything right. Hand them the felt pen so they can correct the drawing as they wish. Encourage the participant to talk about any insights, thoughts or feelings they are taking away from the session.

■What if people get in too deep?

Both adults and children will tend to work at the depth and level at which they feel comfortable. If they feel safe with you, they will go deeper. Feeling safe means that they are confident you will be able to accurately empathise and understand them without judging or misinterpreting in ways we discussed earlier. If someone has felt deeply about something they have drawn or spoken about, then make sure you allow a really good length of time at the end of the session to reflect on this. That said, if you worry that someone is going away too distressed, and you are not a trained counsellor or therapist, then make sure you consult your supervisor.

■It's vital you only work within your limits of competence and get appropriate supervision

It is always good to have a supervisor who is a registered counsellor or therapist with years of experience, with whom you can talk about your work. (This is common practice in psychotherapy and counselling.) A ratio of one supervision session for every six sessions you have with a participant is a good ratio. Supervision is an excellent place to take your own feelings about something you have found troubling in your work with a participant. The supervisor will also give you vital feedback in terms of your interventions and ways of being with the participant. Supervision will dramatically affect the quality and safety of your work. (Use the British Association for Counselling and Psychotherapy's directory to find a supervisor in your area.) In addition, always have someone who is trained in psychological treatment to whom you can refer on if you feel out of your depth in any way.

■Summary of safety rules

1 Never assume that you know what something means to the participant. It may mean something seemingly obvious to you, whilst actually meaning something entirely different to the participant.
2 Never use closed meanings (e.g. a hill is always a breast). Always ask the participant what something means for them.
3 Before you empathise, if you are at all unsure about the meaning of an image or drawing, ask for more information. Never assume.
4 Watch out for hidden incorrect assumptions in the choice of words you use in response to an image or drawing.
5 Make sure you ask open, not closed, questions.
6 Avoid 'Why?' questions.
7 Know how to work with half-said statements and unfinished sentences.
8 Process your own emotional pain, trauma and loss. Go to see a counsellor to work through your own emotional baggage. You will be a far more effective practitioner if you do.
9 Always allow time for reflection at the end of a session.
10 Know your limits of competence and refer on as appropriate.
11 If possible, have a supervisor to whom you can talk and get feedback on your work.

About sandplay and how to use it

The sandplay technique was first devised by Margaret Lowenfeld in 1927 and then taught at the Institute of Child Psychology from 1931. Sandplay is for all ages. Some people mistakenly think it is just for children. Sandplay, a 3D art form, is an incredible technique for working through feelings and addressing emotional baggage. It enables people both to access and convey complex emotional experiences, self-states and sense impressions and to present an in-depth *multisensorial* view of key aspects of their inner or outer world.

Participants choose from a whole range of miniature objects (usually small toys or little ornaments), which ideally are arranged on shelves. They then place their chosen objects in the sandtray in order to symbolise something in their inner or outer world. They can mould the sand to create a landscape on which to place the objects. Ask the participant whether they want to work in wet sand or dry sand. Ideally, you need two sandtrays, one with wet sand and one with dry sand.

Sandplay is also known as the 'world technique' as ideally practitioners have miniatures on their shelves to represent most things in the world. This is a tall order and you can get completely addicted to boot sales for a while. That said, you need to have a range of miniatures from the following categories:

- Transport (must include emergency service vehicles as well as trains, planes, helicopters, cars, buses, etc.)
- People (to include figures of aggression or cruelty, figures of love or warmth, mythical figures such as trolls, witches and fairies, and family members)
- People in professions (policeman, nurse, lollipop person, teacher, etc.)
- Monsters
- Farmyard animals
- Jungle animals
- Buildings (houses, prison, fort, etc.)
- Furniture (bath, bed, armchair, toilet, etc.)
- Outside man-made world objects (gate, road, fence, etc.)
- Outside natural world (trees, flowers, hedge, stones, shells, cliffs)

Children often use the sandbox as their theatre. It is the frame or forum for the action they play out. Because of the sand, they can bury things or bomb things, and everything stands up easily. When they wet the sand, they can mould it into a landscape or building, a fort, or an island or cave, so the miniatures can be given an immediate environment or stage all set for the action of the story.

■ More benefits of using sandplay as an expressive medium

- Unlike painting, the miniatures are easily moveable so the participant can rearrange them, try out different placings, add things or take things out, until they are entirely satisfied that they have conveyed exactly what they want to.
- Through sandplay, the participant can convey multiple meanings and different aspects of the same experience simultaneously. They can, for example, convey feelings about 'my father' and show many different aspects, different feelings, different personal meanings of 'father' simultaneously.
- Through sandplay, the participant can convey the feeling tone of his inner world with exactitude through the complex relation of forms, the moulding and shaping of the sand, the choice of the miniatures, in terms of their size, symbol, colour, and then their positioning and placing, distance from each other, height, depth.
- A sandpicture also provides the practitioner with a very clear view of the participant's world. They can really imagine themselves into that world, which is shown so clearly in the sandbox. They can ask themselves, what would it be like for me to be in this world, e.g. a world where everyone is looking away from everyone else, or a world where there is no green, no life, no coziness, no place of sanctuary, or a world of endless battle?

- The sandplay technique can offer a real sense of safety as an expressive medium. This is because few people have negative associations around playing in the sand, as opposed to, say, bad school experiences with music or art.

■How to introduce the participant to sandplay

Show the participant the miniatures and the sandbox. Put your hands in the sandbox to show the blue on the bottom, which can represent water. Demonstrate how you can wet and then mould the sand into a building, a wall, a dam, so that you have a setting. Show the participant how to place miniatures in the setting to convey something or to enact something.

The sandbox itself should measure about $23 \times 29 \times 3$ inches ($57 \times 72 \times 7$ cm).

Further reading

Aziz-Zadeh, L., Liew, S.-L. and Dandekar, F. (2012) Exploring the neural correlates of visual creativity. *Social Cognitive and Affective Neuroscience* 8: 475–480.

Durante, D. and Dunson, B. (2016) Bayesian inference and testing of group differences in brain networks. *Bayesian Analysis.* Available at: https://projecteuclid.org/euclid.ba/1479179031.

You, your relationships, your life

■Objective

This exercise is designed to give the participant a clear sense of their core beliefs about self, other people and life in general. Perception is highly coloured by these core beliefs. You can easily ascertain someone's core beliefs by asking them to finish three sentences:

- I am . . .
- Other people are . . .
- Life is . . .

If a person's core beliefs are negative, it is really useful to know this so that they can be addressed and worked through, in order to prevent good experiences and relationships in the present being spoiled or damaged. Take, for example, a person who holds the following negative core beliefs:

- **I am** rubbish.
- **People are** untrustworthy. They will only let me down in the end.
- **Life is** a kind of punishment.

Without addressing his core beliefs, this person is likely to have a lot of misery in his life, and either 'shrink from the world or do battle with it' (Bowlby, 1979). The first step to change is awareness and this is what is offered in this exercise.

■Instructions to give the participant

Without thinking about it, quickly fill in the picture frames entitled, 'I am . . . ', 'Other people are . . . ', 'Life is . . . '. Fill in all three boxes for each category. Write down or draw the first things that come into your mind. In the 'Other people are . . . ' section, you can use '**Some** people are . . . ' as a sentence starter if you prefer. You can choose to write their names next to the appropriate box or not.

After completion

What have you learnt about yourself, the people in your life and your views about life from doing this? Is it clarification of something already known or an 'Aha!' experience, a new insight? How do you think you came to feel this way? What big life events do you think have informed what you have drawn or written? Often key events in childhood heavily inform our core beliefs. Can you think of any from your childhood? When you look at what you have written, is there anything you would like to change in your life as a result? What would you need to do to make these things happen?

■Development – The Unfinished Sentence game

The follow-on to this exercise will again give the participant a clearer sense of their core beliefs about self, others and life in general. Simply ask the participant to finish the sentences below and say the first thing that comes into their mind. (They can say it, write it or draw it.)

If the participant is speaking out loud, ask them to close their eyes. Some people like to lie down (as if free-associating on the proverbial Freudian couch).

- I like it when people . . .
- I love it when people . . .

- I don't like it when people . . .
- I am frightened when . . .
- I get angry when . . .
- I feel good about myself when . . .
- I feel like rubbish when I . . .
- I wish people knew that I . . .
- I hate people who . . .
- I like people who . . .
- I respect people who . . .
- I am unkind to myself when . . .
- I am kind to myself when . . .

Write down their answers as the participant speaks (unless *they* have chosen to write down their answers). Now say back to the participant what they have written, pausing between each statement so they can take it in and comment. Ask the participant what they have learnt about themselves from doing the exercise.

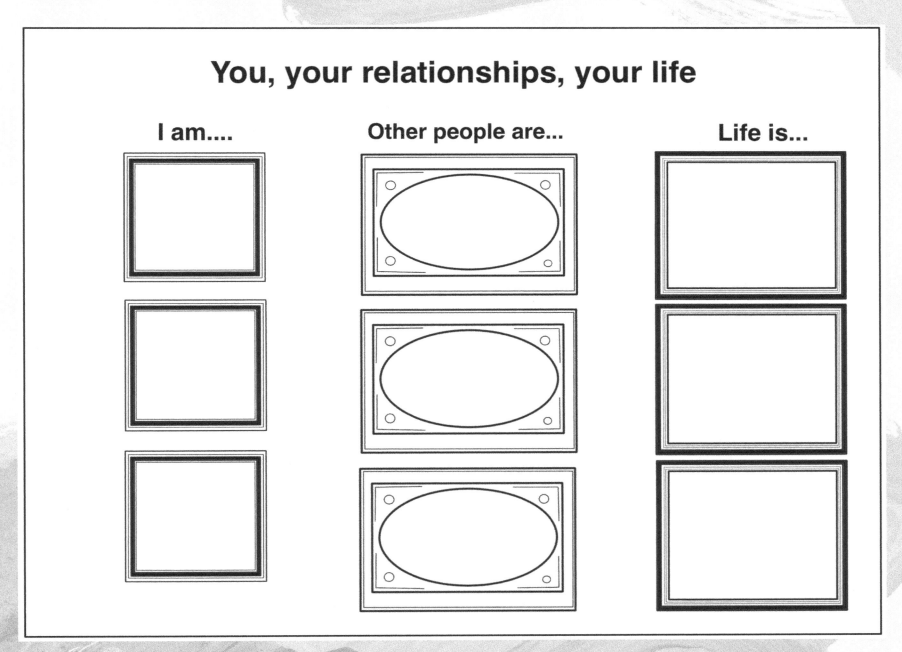

Figure 1.1

Encouragers and discouragers in my life (past and present)

■Objective

Some people have a hard life in part because they have known too much discouragement and too little encouragement. As a result, they find it difficult to motivate themselves, to believe in themselves or to grasp opportunities. When the criticism comes from significant people in your life, they can leave a residue in your mind in the form of self-talk. Self-talk refers to what you say to yourself inside your head. Negative self-talk is so powerful it can blight a person's will, determination, motivation, capacity to learn and self-esteem. It can be so damning that it is far worse than how you would ever talk to another person, e.g. 'You are so stupid', 'You are useless', 'You never get anything right'. On the other hand, self-talk can be encouraging: 'Never mind, that didn't work, but I know you'll get there if you just keep going with this'. Encouraging self-talk is a key aspect of resilience and a vital factor in a person's capacity to enjoy a successful and deeply satisfying life. This exercise is designed to heighten the participant's awareness of their self-talk, because this is a key first step towards positive change in this important area of psychological health and to seek out people who encourage now, if these have been lacking in the past.

■Instructions to give the participant

Think back over your life to the people who have encouraged or discouraged you and write the names of encouragers on the stars and the discouragers on the thumbs down. You might also like to write the psychological messages or core beliefs you think each of them has left you with, e.g. 'You can make it' or 'Don't do anything special with your life'. You can also draw more stars and thumbs down if you need to. When you have finished, stand back and look. Do you seem to have had more discouragers or encouragers in your life? Which of all the people in your gallery are still influencing your self-talk – what you say to yourself inside your head? It may be a person you haven't seen for years, or they may be dead, and yet they are still having a big effect on you for better or worse.

■Development – The inner critic

If it seems that the participant has 'internalised' lots of discouraging voices, explore with them what it feels like to live with the inner critic triggering negative self-talk for too much of the time.

You might like to ask them to make an image of their inner critic in clay. Then ask them to speak to their inner critic or do what they want to do to them. Alternatively, they may like to write their inner critic a short letter entitled 'What it's been like living with you inside my head'. One way to deal with inner critics is to make a tape recording of what they say. The participant can then have a very vivid and concrete example of their negative self-talk and decide whether or not they choose to listen to it anymore, or just 'turn it off'.

'Thought stoppage' is an excellent technique which is very relevant here. Explain to the participant that they can stop thinking something if it is not helping them (a revelation for some people). So, if a critical voice pops up in their head, they can say out loud 'Stop', 'Calm', or bang the table and say 'Enough'.

It can also help people to know that a negative or critical thought can prolong a negative feeling or mood state, so if they stop themselves thinking the negative thought they can often change what they are feeling. We really do have the power to stop listening to an inner critic and to think of something else, or even bring to mind some lovely memory. This is a skill well worth practising. Ask the participant to think of a few key lovely memories, or bring to mind encouraging people, which they can use as a resource in this way.

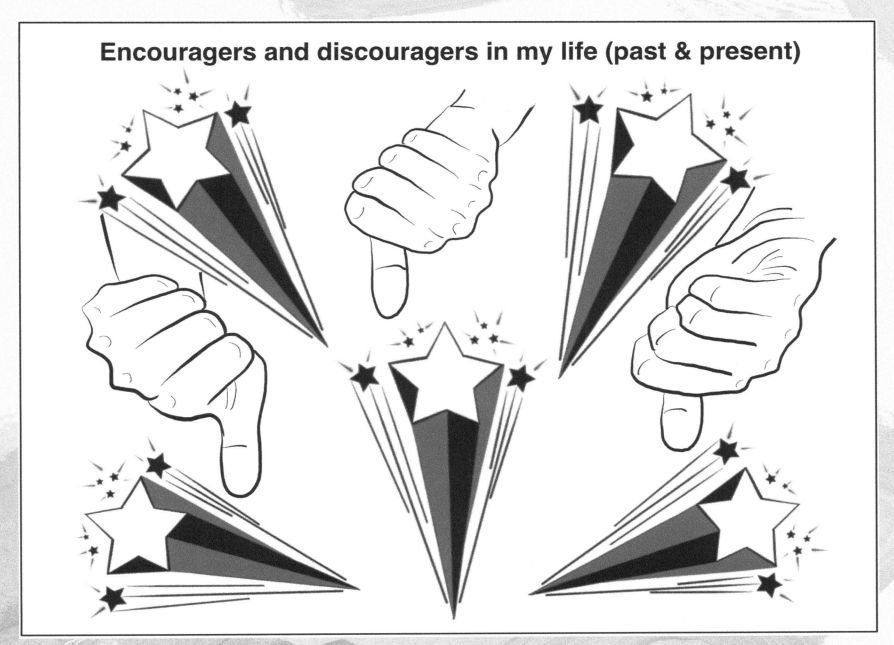

Encouragers and discouragers in my life (past & present)

Figure 1.2

People in your life as gardens

■Objective

This exercise provides the participant with a vehicle to heighten their awareness of the emotional atmospheres and energies that the various people they know or have known bring into their life.

■Instructions to give the participant

From the picture, pick a 'garden circle' for each of the people who are or have had a big effect on your life, for better or worse. Draw the gardens of these people. For example, are they a garden with colourful flowers but with hidden thorns and stinging nettles? Or are they a rich, luscious garden, albeit a bit wild and overgrown? Are they full of flowers but with a big desolate place in the middle of the garden? Or do they have a large electric fence or a 'Keep Out' sign?

Write the names of the people you have chosen under the appropriate garden circle.

Then, if you like, imagine yourself in each of the gardens. If it were real life what would you feel if you spent time in there? What would you do in the garden? What would you change or leave exactly as it is?

Is there some action you may want to take in your personal or professional life as a result of doing this exercise? If not now, then when? Next month? Next year? If some actions feel scary, what support would you need to have to bring about positive change, so that you don't keep putting off improving the quality of your life?

■Development – People in your life as animals

This is a remarkably simple exercise and yet it often brings participants some new and important awareness about the people in their lives (past or present).

■Instructions to give the participants

On one big sheet of paper, draw the key people in your life as a group of animals. Draw quickly without too much thinking. Show the expression on each of their faces. Draw yourself as one of the animals. Then step back and look at what you have drawn. What have you learnt about yourself and them in terms of the sizes, shapes and positions you have chosen, and the groupings, togetherness and separateness? Is there anything you want to change in your life when you look at what you have drawn? If you wish, you can draw another picture to show how you would like the group of animals to be. Is there any constructive change you could make as a result of your learning from the picture? You can repeat the exercise drawing the key people in your childhood as a group of animals.

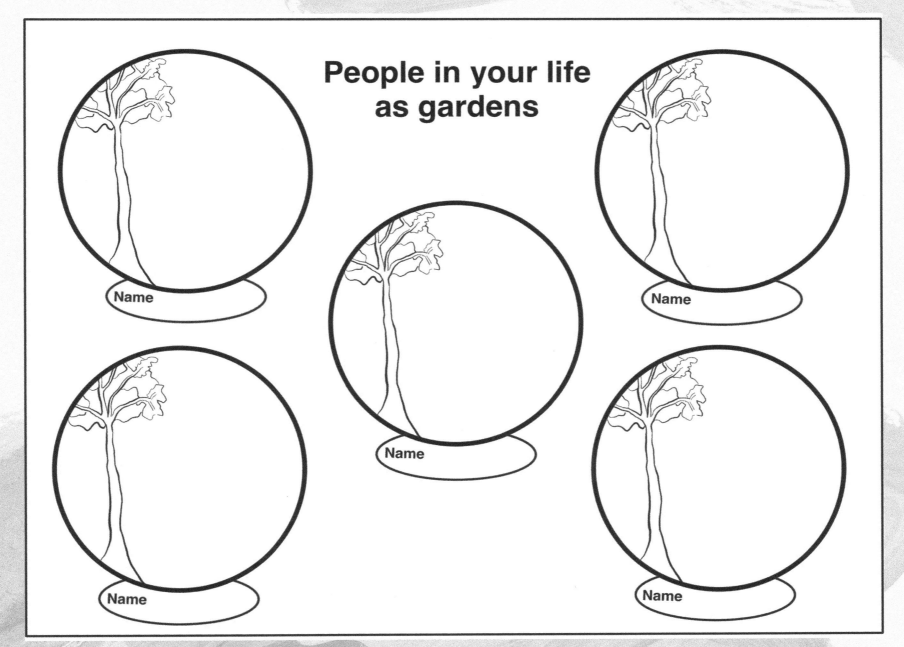

Figure 1.3

The cocktail party

▪Objective

This exercise is to enable participants of all ages to take a long, hard look at people in their lives, past or present, and consider whether these people are adding to their quality of life or not. Without such reflection time, it is all too easy to drift along in life, investing too much in draining or destructive relationships, and too little in relationships that are truly life-affirming. It is easy to be caught in the grip of painful relational experiences from the past. These can continue to influence our lives negatively until they are processed or worked through in the present. Focused reflection as provided by this exercise can be a vital first step for a person to improve their life with more enriching human capital.

▪Instructions to give the participants

Think of the people in your life (past and present) who are, or have been, very significant to you in one way or another. There may be some people with whom you have not had very much contact, and yet they have markedly influenced your life for the better (e.g. an inspiring teacher) or worse (e.g. a bully). In this picture, all the people in your life have come together at one big cocktail party. They have divided themselves into groups of like-minded people.

Think of each significant person in your life and write their name on one of the figures in the group that most applies to them. If someone you know falls into more than one group (because they have different sides to them), just write their name on as many figures as you need. When you have finished, stand back and look at what you have drawn. What does your peopled life look like? Do you have enough people in the positive groups? If not, what can you do to ensure you spend more time with people who are good for you and less time with people who cause you stress? How

much of your life is richly resourced with lovely, inspiring, warm people and how much of your life is being spoiled by relationships that are not enabling you to use life well?

▪Development – Childhood figures

If the participant is an adult, ask them to do the same exercise simply focusing on their childhood figures. Alternatively, they may explore through sandplay and/or the use of miniatures.

▪Instructions to give the participant

Find objects in the room or sandplay miniatures (see 'About sandplay and how to use it' in the Introduction) to represent key people in your childhood. Place them all on a piece of paper or sandbox with an object to represent you as the child you felt you were. After you have done this, say what you have learned from your choice of objects or miniatures in sand or in paper. You may like to rearrange them as you would have liked your childhood to be, by adding people or removing them from the paper. Is there anything you can learn from this about how you want to live your life now?

The cocktail party

The critics and discouragers

The inspirers

The 'poor me' people

The warm and lovely

The drainers and takers

The threatening/dangerous

The grey and dull

The encouragers

The angry volcanoes

The mistrusted

The loved and lost

Figure 1.4

Your relationships as walls, bridges, comfortable sofas and take off

■Objective

This exercise focuses on the important issue of emotional closeness and distance, and relationships through which you develop as a person, those which you do not, and those where things are not great between you but you have the emotional energy to want to try to repair them. So, the exercise is intended to support the participant to reflect on their relationship life as a whole, and consider necessary action rather than just becoming complacent, sticking with the status quo, or with relationships that sap confidence, life force or feelings of self-worth.

■Instructions to give the participants

Look at the picture. Read the descriptions below to see what the images represent.

Walls

These are people in your life (past or present) you've given up on in some way. You may have shut them out or they may have shut you out, or you walked away from them or they walked away from you and did not return. You no longer contemplate the possibility of approach and repair. You may think it would lead to yet more rejection and more heartache. Nevertheless, they were/are very significant people in your life.

Bridges

These are people in your life you're still in contact with, but from whom you are emotionally distant or in conflict with in some way. Perhaps with one or more of these people there has been a misconnection, a falling out, or a general distancing over time. But you would like to get closer to them. You want to find a way to walk over the bridge (metaphorically speaking) and resolve any unfinished business you have with this person.

Comfortable sofas

These are people in your life towards whom, for the most part, you feel really affectionate. You feel secure in their affection or love for you. These are good relationships, important to you and likely to stay this way over time. They may not be particularly exciting relationships, but they are warm and basically good. They enrich or have enriched your life. Even if one of these people is dead or you haven't seen them for years, they are, as Bruce Perry (2002) says, 'A gift that keeps on giving'.

Take off

These are exciting relationships (they may be a group of people of which you are a member, or just one person). The energy between you is sometimes exhilarating. You feel at one with this person or group, share energy states, and feel that together you cango flying in some way. You develop as a person through knowing this person or group.

Having read the descriptions, write on the appropriate image the names of the people in your life with whom you feel you have this type of relationship. A person's name can appear on more than one type of image. After you have finished, stand back and look at what you have drawn.

Which of the images seem particularly significant to you? Do you, for example, have a lot of bridges or wall-type relationships and fewer take offs and comfy sofas? Is there any action you want to take with any of the people you have named? Perhaps an important conversation you've been putting off with one, or giving another some feedback? Are you withholding some appreciation and gratitude? If so, how could you dare to express this? If there are people you have named on the walls, what do you miss about each of these people? And what are you relieved about in terms of them no longer being a part of your life? Are you sure that a part of you doesn't want to try to repair?

■Development – Discussion: Relationship repair

If the participant has drawn a lot of bridges, help them to think about what is stopping them getting on and walking across the bridge to connect with the other person. It can help to do a rehearsal of how they could open up a dialogue with these people. Or place an empty chair opposite them and ask them to imagine the person is sitting in the chair. Ask them to speak to them, using the support of unfinished sentences spoken by yourself, such as 'What I need from you is . . . ' or 'What I need you to know is . . . '. Sometimes it may be appropriate to help the participant to consider in more depth a 'Wall relationship' which, out of hopelessness or bitterness, they may have just written off. This is particularly relevant if a person's picture is full of walls and too comfy sofas and take offs.

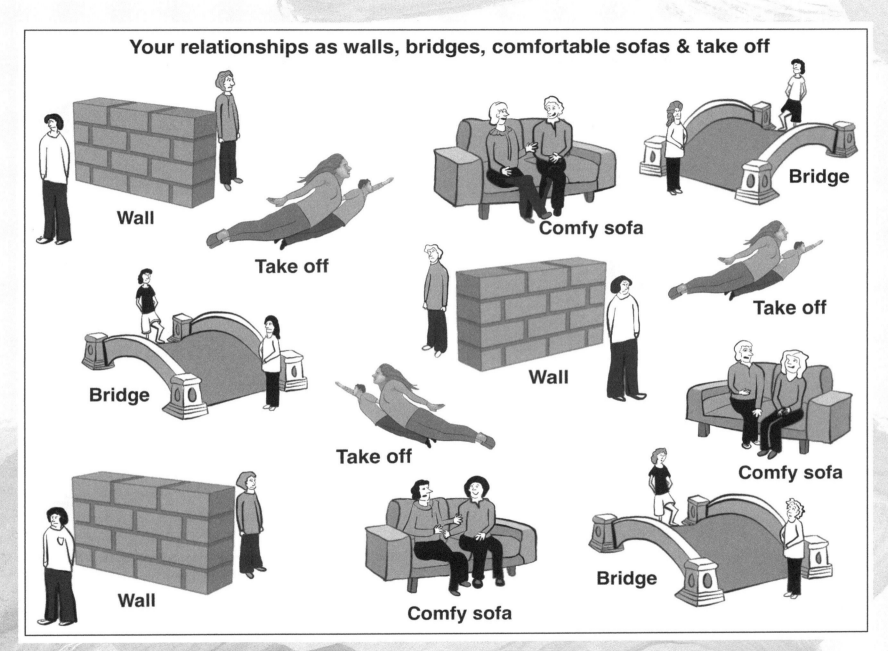

Your relationships as walls, bridges, comfortable sofas & take off

Wall

Take off

Comfy sofa

Bridge

Bridge

Wall

Take off

Comfy sofa

Wall

Comfy sofa

Bridge

Figure 1.5

Museum of too alone

■Objective

The novelist Doris Lessing said that if you've known bleakness in childhood it never leaves you. That said, experiences of desolation or intense loneliness *can* be modified by talking about them with someone who is good at listening and who helps you to make sense of them and work through them. This exercise can offer an important context for some of that quality reflection time. It is vital, however, that the practitioner has direct felt experience of such pain from their own life, rather than having to shut themselves off from those feelings. Without this, they will be unable to offer accurate empathy to ensure the participant feels safe enough to open up and share their experiences.

■Instructions to give the participants

Draw and/or write in the six exhibit boxes in the museum of too alone the most important times in your life when you felt very alone and no one was there to help you. Write the age you were at the time (or just write 'child', adolescent', 'adult'). Write some of the feelings you felt in each box. If you prefer, just circle the feelings you felt from the list on the side of the page. You don't need to fill in all six boxes, but you can add more exhibits if the six is not enough.

When you have finished, step back and look at your museum. What do you feel about what you have drawn or written? How are these times still impacting on you in your life now, and how you feel today about yourself, other people and life in general? Could you have asked for help at the time? If so, what stopped you? What does this tell you about your relationship to help? Or did you ask for help but got no response?

■Development – Tour of the museum of too alone

Photocopy the museum picture so that it is enlarged to A3 or A2. Ask the participant to choose a figure or object to represent themselves and also one to represent you. The participant and you then move these chosen figures into each exhibit in turn. In this way, you are both revisiting these too-alone experiences as you would exhibits in an actual museum. You act as the first witness, and because you are there this time, it is not a re-traumatising but a re-experiencing, which modifies the original experience. Ask the participant to say the things or do the things they wished they had done or said at the time. This may include speaking to people who were emotionally or physically absent at the time. You can support the process by using the unfinished sentence technique, e.g. 'I felt so alone. What I needed you to know was . . . '

The participant may experience difficulty in finding the words. If so, your figure 'as witness' can speak. Holding the figure that represents you, start sentences like this: 'I am so sorry this happened to you. I can imagine how painful it must have been to have felt . . . ' You may even speak to one of the people in the participant's life whom could have helped but didn't, e.g. 'It was not okay that you left her all alone with that. She was just a little girl.'

Museum of too alone

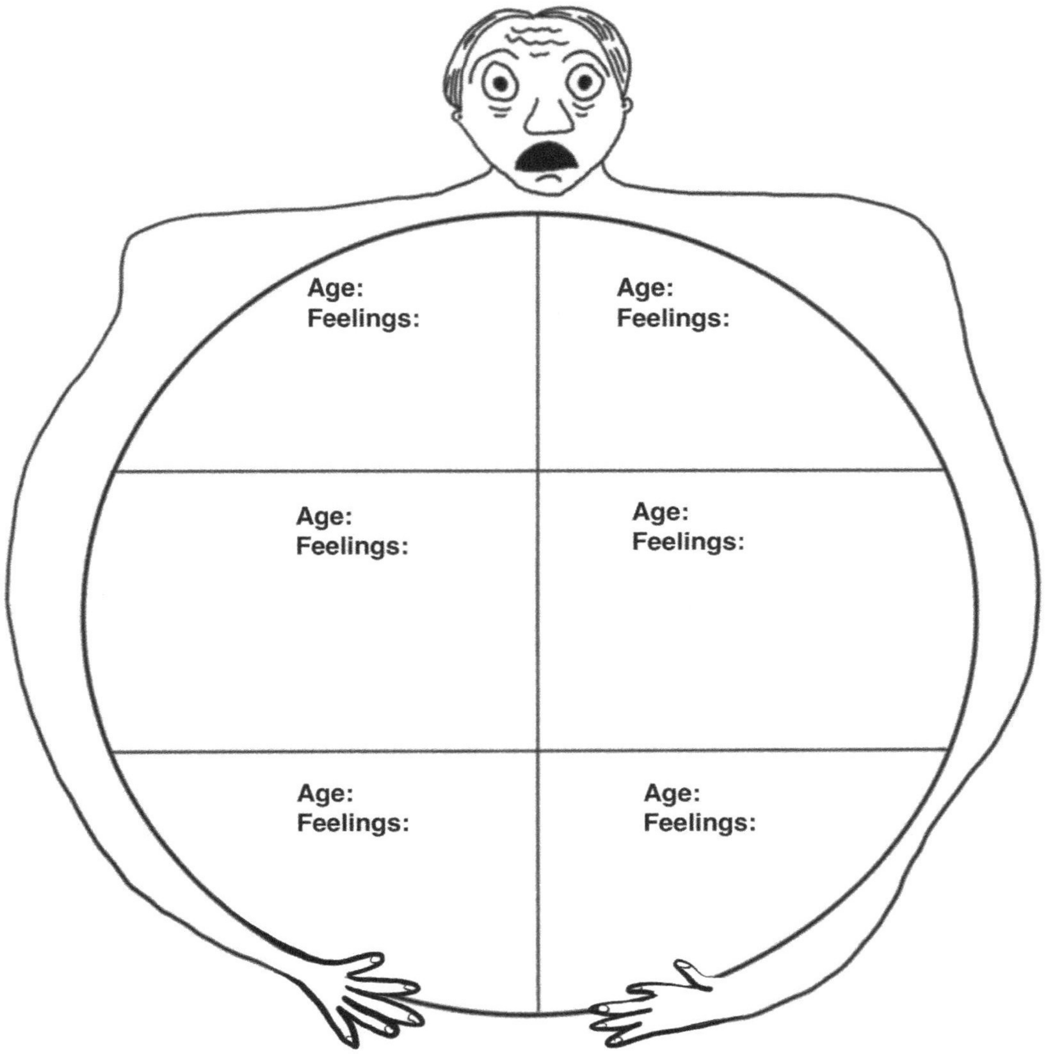

Age: Feelings:	Age: Feelings:
Age: Feelings:	Age: Feelings:
Age: Feelings:	Age: Feelings:

Hopeless
Despair
Heartbroken
Frightened
Terrified
Desolate
Desperate
Useless
Impotent
Wanting to burst into tears
Like your world had ended
Angry
Rage
Full of silent screams
Like giving up
Wanting to die

Figure 1.6

My childhood memories: People as places

■Objective

The exercise actively supports a time for the participant to reminisce on the lovely relationships in their childhood, which continue to enrich their life today and their painful childhood relationships which still impact negatively.

It is now firmly established and backed by thousands of psychological and brain research studies that:

- Childhood relationships have dramatic effects on later-life relationships and mental health.
- Childhood relationships have dramatic effects on physical health and the immune system.
- Childhood relationships dramatically inform the core beliefs people have about themselves, others and life in general.
- Painful childhood relationships can become prototypical for later-life relationships.

(Bellis et al., 2017; Burke Harris, 2015)

One vital step towards preventing painful childhood relationships from spoiling quality of life and damaging psychological and physical health is to speak about them in a safe context in order to work them through (see 'Why work through feelings about relationships?' in the Introduction). A safe context means someone listening with warmth, unconditional positive regard and accurate empathy and helping you make sense of what has happened. This can only happen when a practitioner has sufficiently worked through their *own* painful childhood relationships at some point in therapy or counselling or with some other emotionally available adult and so is not defending against their own painful feelings.

■Instructions to give the participant

Think of your childhood relationships. Then look at the picture. Who in your childhood took you, metaphorically speaking, to the various places in this picture? Write their name next to the appropriate place. You may find that you write the same names next to several different places because you have had very mixed experiences with these people. Draw in other places if they are not represented in the way you need. Then next to the 'core belief' under each of the places you've chosen, write what you think you've learnt about yourself or other people and/or life in general from this relationship. Simple, short sentences are best, starting, 'I am . . . ', 'Other people are . . . ', or 'Life is . . . '.

Example

- Person who took you into the dark threatening place – Core belief: 'I am rubbish'.
- Person who took you to the beach (metaphorically speaking) – Core belief: 'I enjoy life'.

Now stand back and look at the picture and how you have changed it. Of all that you see now, which childhood relationships do you think brought you the most pain and which brought you the most pleasure or gratitude?

■Development – Take back your power

This is a useful follow-up exercise designed to help people who, due to painful childhood experiences, find themselves in their life now all too easily moving into feelings of impotence, defeat or hopelessness even with relatively minor stressors. Ask the participant to draw a picture or do a sandplay to represent people in their childhood who made them feel powerless, worthless or not good enough. Then ask them to speak to each person in turn. Ask them to use the unfinished sentence technique, e.g. 'I hated you because . . . ', 'You didn't realise that I needed . . . ', 'I want you to know that . . . '. The sandbox is like a mini theatre in which to enact mini psychodramas like this safely and in a contained way. The participant can also move the figures around as they choose, bury them, throw them out, etc. and hence feel like they are taking back their power by addressing what they could not address as a child. We know from evidence-based research that expressing 'empowered anger' in this way is a key part of the healing process (Lane et al., 2015).

Example

Tom, age 25, speaks in sandplay to a cruel teacher he suffered when aged five. In the sandbox Tom had chosen a three-headed dragon to be the teacher. With the miniature figures he chose, he said to her, 'I dreaded every day at school with you. I had no voice. I did not let my parents know. I didn't know I could ask for help. But I will speak to you now. You should never have gone near children . . . Your cold-as-ice mood, day in, day out, was lethal. I want to break you in two because I felt broken by you. How dare you take out all your anger on the children in your care? You are an emotional abuser. I still suffer fear and shame in my life because of you.' Having spoken to her, he said he felt an enormous relief and a feeling of taking back his power after 20 years!

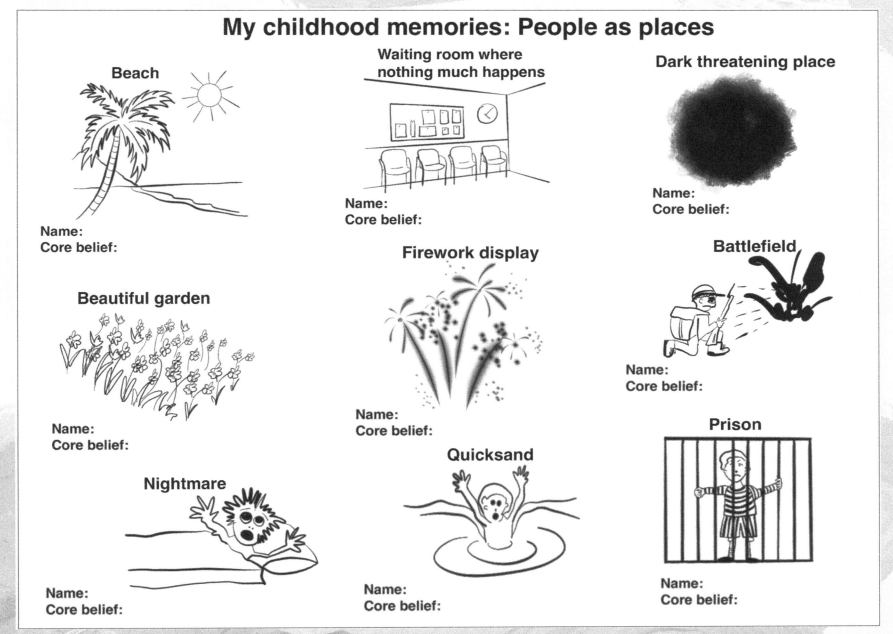

Figure 1.7

Relationship riches

■Objective

This exercise aims to enable the participant to consider the people in their life in terms of the relationship riches and human resources they have. The structured reflection time is designed to enable the participant to savour the people who enrich their life with such important things as inspiration, encouragement, empathy and playfulness. Hopefully, with heightened awareness, where such relationship riches are thin on the ground, the participant may feel more motivated to seek out new friends or extend their social network in creative ways.

■Instructions to give the participant

Think of the people in past or present that have enriched your life. Write the names of the people who first come to mind when you look at each picture. Maybe you no longer see these people or perhaps they have died, and yet those people are still a profoundly positive presence in your mind. So, in this sense you are still 'calling on them' in your mind for these most important human resources. You may want to write more than one name on some of the pictures.

From doing the exercise, what have you learned about how you value particular people in your life, past or present? Do you have gaps for certain activities, or in terms of people to whom you feel you could easily turn for support when the going gets tough? How could you 'people' your life in different ways to ensure you are not missing out on these important relationship riches?

■Development – The wonder of positive shared activity

This exercise focuses on the qualitatively different energetic charge of 'doing things together' compared with doing things on your own; how shared energy can often give birth to some amazing new ideas, new adventure or new way of being that would not have been possible through solo activity. Ask the participant to share with you the times when they felt they were thriving, flying high, being really creative as a result of some shared or group activity. This important reminiscing may inspire them to seek out more enriching shared activities for themselves in the future.

If this exercise has opened up a rich vein for the participant, you could consider progressing to an exercise called 'The social capital in your life'. Ask the participant the following: 'Who in your life do you really appreciate in terms of the following qualities?'

- Good team player
- Capacity to inspire you
- Great listener
- Always there when you need them
- Ability to give you really good advice with a problem
- Capacity to compromise/negotiate
- Capacity to have fun and play
- Sense of humour
- Capacity to help you think really clearly when you are stressed out
- Capacity to calm you down
- Capacity to give you hope
- Capacity to make you feel safe in the world

Relationship riches

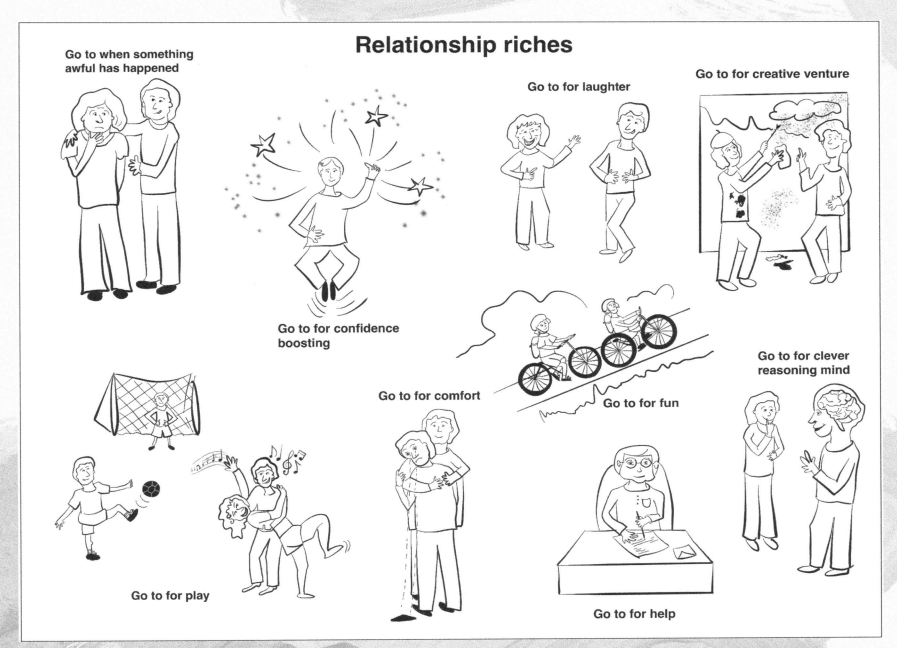

Figure 1.8

Further reading

Bellis, M. A., Hardcastle, K., Ford, K., Hughes, K., Ashton, K., Quigg, Z. and Butler, N. (2017) Does continuous trusted adult support in childhood impart life-course resilience against adverse childhood experiences – a retrospective study on adult health-harming behaviours and mental well-being. *BMC Psychiatry*, 23 March, 17(1): 110.

Burke Harris, N. (2015) Summit – adverse childhood experience and toxic stress. A public health crisis. The Area Health Education Center of Washington State University.

Lane, R. D, Ryan, L., Nadel, L. and Greenberg, L. (2015) Memory reconsolidation, emotional arousal and the process of change in psychotherapy: New insights from brain science. *Behav. Brain Sci.*, January.

Dead, depriving, draining, disappointing relationships

■Essential theory

It takes considerable artistry in life to know when something is finished.

(Polster, 1987)

■About dead relationships

One may find oneself enlivened and the sense of one's own being enhanced by the other, or one may experience the other as deadening and impoverishing.

(Laing, 1990)

Dead relationships are those in which neither party is thriving. On a day-to-day basis, too much of the energy between the two people is disinterested energy. There can be genuine affection, but the relationship has too little music, so to speak. Over time, emotional sterility can spread, suffocating any possibility of passionate or meaningful exchange (emotional, intellectual or sexual). The two people no longer have a basic curiosity about the other or any real interest in what the other person might be thinking or feeling. There are no longer any meaningful, honest conversations based on 'how is life for you, and how is life for you with me?' Too much has become privately guarded. Innermost thoughts and feelings go un-shared so the relationship is kept at a nice comfortable level. Both parties have closed in on themselves and there is no real desire for a better connection. In short, the relationship has lost its soul. In some cases, it may never have had it in the first place.

In other relationships there is the sense of just drifting along, 'going nowhere together'. As Woody Allen says: 'A relationship is like a shark. It has to constantly move forward or it dies.' (Allen, 1977) Some people have the courage to speak about this to each other, but others do not. Many people hope to develop and thrive as a result of being in an intimate relationship. If this does not happen there can be a deep sense of disappointment and even betrayal: 'Surely, the deal was that if I invested so much in this relationship with you, I would develop and move on in my own life, and now I'm even more stuck than ever before'. It is also the feeling of drifting, deadness, not developing, that is often a catalyst for having affairs. Living life outside the relationship begins, because the person has given up on there ever being life within it.

Relationships when one party wants to enliven and deepen the relationship and the other doesn't really care

These are relationships where one person is quite happy with the comfort zone and to live within a narrow band of mild, safe feelings, whereas the other person wants something more. The latter is acutely aware of what they are missing together, and of how neither of them is really developing in the relationship.

Sometimes in these relationships, one person at the start may have been thriving, only for their life force to be stifled by being with the other, as conveyed in the following poem:

Little Life

With you,
I have to watch
I don't get tangled up
In the limitations you put on yourself.
I have to see that your stop signs
Don't become my stop signs

And that I don't grow cold
By what you've chosen not to feel.
But in the face of your avid affair with safe and known,
I can't keep the bleakness out of our bed.

(The author)

So how does a relationship move into drifting or deadness?

- Too many failed attempts at connecting, too many reachings out that went wrong, too many expressions of hurt that went unheard, too many unspoken feelings.
- Both parties have an unspoken agreement never to disagree. In their attempts to keep everything nice they never allow themselves any expression of anger or resentment. Some say, 'We have a wonderful relationship. We never argue.' They flatly deny any destructive thoughts or impulses towards their partner. This is often because such impulses are too dangerous to think about. The result is soon the death of all passionate feelings in the relationship. In the end, unexpressed anger can make both love and sex impossible. One man told his partner, 'Disagreement isn't in my vocabulary'. He had had a mother who could not manage his anger or excitement, so he had learnt to repress his passion. After a year, their sexual engagement was at an end.
- A build-up of unexpressed feelings of anger and resentment has blighted the lifeblood of the relationship. In other words, there is a hothouse of unspoken feelings underneath the 'niceness' that act as a drain on the relationship's energy. Both parties behave pleasantly to each other on the surface, but when they have collected enough resentments, they leave, by having an affair or by walking out. One woman, not understanding why her husband eventually left her to live with his exciting mistress, said, 'I was so considerate. I never made demands. I tried so hard never to upset him and yet he left me.' It is a tragic waste of many relationships to be deadened in this way when there are lots of excellent safe and structured ways of expressing resentments in close relationships (see 'The art of relationship' chapter in the book).

- When a couple delude themselves into thinking that apart from a few petty annoyances they have only loving feelings for each other, there is a denial or lack of understanding about the human condition. The reality is of course that where there is strong love, the hurts, when they inevitably happen, will be equally strong simply by virtue of the fact that this person matters so much. Where the hurt is not expressed and worked through, it can move into a wall of hate.

So why do the two people continue with their relationship when it is drifting or dead?

- The comfort and safety of familiarity coupled with fears of being alone. That said, if one person dares to leave a dead relationship, fears are often unfounded and they find a new lease of life. As Ibsen wrote: 'When we dead awaken, we find we've never lived'. But it takes courage, of course.
- The hope that they can improve their relationship. Yet all too often deadness eats away at the very life force of the relationship, which blights any hope of change. Others will one day have a sudden realisation that they are living with and sleeping next to someone they no longer love. In protection of their own life force, they find within themselves the courage to leave. As one man in such a relationship remarked, 'I realised I just had to leave when I knew I would rather have a meal with a stranger than with my wife'.
- They have no model of any other sort of relationship. In childhood they have been members of 'Families in which there is no friendship among the members, will lack the glue of soul to hold them together' (Moore, 1994).
- Staying in dead relationships can be the result of too many parent – child connections which were weak, banal, impersonal or formal and where the parent's love was inhibited or family culture of politeness, formality or 'stiff upper lip' inhibition and lack of spontaneity around expressions of love. The parent may rarely if ever say to the child, 'I love you' or 'You're lovely' and so love is confined to small gestures and small affectionate acts, such as through offerings of food.

What can be done?

The exercises can be really useful to heighten awareness of this aspect of a relationship. They may galvanise the person to talk about and confront the drifting and the deadness to voice and acknowledge their discontent with the sameness, the growing feelings of alienation, the loss of interest in the other. 'What we might do differently' can then be looked at and put into action from the smallest details to the most dramatic changes, the latter to act as a necessary jolt into a wide range of relational options (see 'The art of relationship' chapter on how this can be done). That said, time with a couple therapist can really help, too.

■About depriving relationships

In emotionally depriving relationships there is a lack of all the things that nourish human beings: warmth, appreciation, good listening, empathy and curiosity in the other. As a result of this scarcity, the emotionally deprived person often waits for the other person to give them some small show of love or appreciation. Metaphorically speaking, they are locked in 'waiting for the sun to shine', in the form of a smile, a touch, an affectionate statement. They can end up trying so hard to please their partner, having to earn or buy the smallest sign of love and affection.

When someone is locked in a relationship with a person who is emotionally depriving, it is easy to mistake rarities for pearls. In other words, if they get a compliment, a protestation of love, or occasionally a present, they can feel deeply grateful. But sadly this 'intermittent reinforcement' just feeds their belief that it's all right to stay. For too long they tolerate the other person's walls of silence, sulking, emotional coldness, angry outbursts, criticism and put-downs.

In return they may find themselves trying to be 'nice' and reasonable, stifling their own feelings and reactions, complying with the other person's wishes and putting up with far too much without protest, things that other people would never dream of tolerating. If they are convinced that one day the other person will leave them, 'being good' and being compliant is an important way of buying time against that fateful day. After all, any expression of anger on their part

may risk the sun going in again, may risk a return of the unbearable distance between them, or may risk losing what little good they do have together.

Another form of the depriving relationship is the affair. Many affairs promise so much, but in reality give so little: snatched time, last-minute cancellations, being regularly 'de-prioritised', and having someone who can never really be there for you. But this can feel far more preferable to no relationship at all for people who fall for the allure of emotionally depriving relationships or dread life without being part of a love duet.

Trying to make someone love you who isn't good at loving

It is very common for a person who puts up with emotionally depriving relationships to think that if they just love this person (often in all manner of overgenerous, self-sacrificing ways) they will be able eventually to 'repair' them. Time and time again, this unfortunate misplaced hope and wishful thinking ends in deep disappointment and the harsh realisation that their loving simply doesn't have this sort of power.

So why do people stay in emotionally depriving relationships?

Sometimes people who have not felt loved in childhood are attracted to people in adulthood who are not good at loving. Freud called this 'repetition compulsion', meaning an unconscious compulsion to repeat the emotional pain of the past. Fairbairn, another famous analyst, talked of the allure of repeating painful childhood relationships because in some sense the person is still trying to work things out. Their life force is locked in their childhood relationships with emotionally depriving parent figures, and also their hope.

Many people who fall for people who cannot love well in the way we have described have experienced a parent who was an 'absent presence'. This means they were physically present, but emotionally absent for too much of the time. Such parent figures did not delight in the child enough to want to engage with him or her in lovely ways on an ongoing basis. Instead they may have engaged too much of the time from duty or obligation. Having someone there out of duty as opposed to love often feels far lonelier than no presence at all.

So what can be done?

The exercises in the book can help people stand back and review this key aspect of their relationship life, past and present. The exercises may help heighten awareness that 'once-in-a-blue-moon' shows of affection are just not enough, that they deserve more than to be treated like this, and to understand that if they are not loved it is not because they are unlovable. Often this awareness is the first step to change. Others may then go into counselling or therapy to enable them to become aware of this replay, to grieve over that original pain and then to feel sufficiently supported to leave.

Childhood example

John, a man in his thirties, had a string of relationships in which his partners would be physically undemonstrative towards him after the honeymoon period was over. In counselling, he realised that he was constantly repeating his relationship with his mother, who had never shown him physical affection as a child. He remembered several instances of her pushing him off her lap. When he had fully mourned this in counselling, he was able to sustain a loving and physically very demonstrative marriage.

■About draining relationships

Some people leave you feeling emotionally drained after you have spent time with them. You may also come away feeling restless, irritable and alone. As you will see, many of these reasons (see below) are to do with lack of emotional range and/or lack of self-awareness in how they are impacting on the other person:

- They talk at you.
- They only want to talk about themselves and are not really interested in you.
- Like a bad piece of music, their voice only has a limited range of notes. Some people, for example, persistently speak with a drone, others are manic and high-pitched.
- They tell you how absolutely everything is 'oh so good' in their life. The lack of any real-life element or more balanced account acts as a barrier to authentic emotional connection between you.

- They are like a 'stuck record' in terms of repeatedly talking about some particular topic, e.g. their aches or pains, their wonderful children, or the same anecdotes over and over.
- They have a narrow emotional range, e.g. they always seem miserable, bitter, depressed, angry, manically happy, etc.
- They frequently put you down.
- They may ask you how you are or what you are doing, but they don't listen to the answer.
- There is a lack of reciprocity; you are the one doing all the listening, showing interest and concern.
- The conversation is dry, devoid of any feeling or personal content.
- They speak largely or entirely of misery: their own, other people's, or how the country is 'going to the dogs', the awful weather, traffic, effects of global warming, etc.
- They are controlling and/or intrusive so that you spend all the time trying to protect/defend yourself.

So why do people stay in emotionally draining relationships?

Many people put up with energy-sapping relationships simply out of habit. Some people are unaware of the level of depletion they feel in terms of being with these people and wrongly label it as some kind of generalised stress or tiredness. Furthermore, it is very difficult to tell a person that they are emotionally draining as this often means you are challenging their very way of being in the world.

There is also the very draining effect of working at a relationship that is actually past saving. It can be easy to believe that so long as you work hard at the relationship it will somehow come back to life. But in actuality, working at something that is so draining is extremely exhausting. To quote Resnick (1998): 'It takes considerable art to know when something is finished'. But for some people an emotionally draining relationship is better than no relationship at all.

So what to do?

Again, the exercises can be useful in heightening awareness for the participant of just how draining and depleting a relationship in their life is. The exercises can help them confront themselves about simply maintaining a status quo: 'Well she is family, so I have to just put up with it' or 'Well I know he is draining but at least I have him as my partner/friend, otherwise I might not find anyone'.

By standing back and looking at how much you are giving in a relationship and how little you are getting can be sobering. The facilitator can help the participant weigh up options, e.g. spending less time with the drainers, or spending a different sort of time (e.g. going to see a film together rather than an hour of listening to their woes), spending more time with people who nourish rather than drain.

■About disappointing relationships

A relationship can start off full of bright hopes and vivid dreams fuelled by influences of the media, images of fairytales and a whole wealth of stories of 'happily ever after'. A plethora of television advertisements show the ecstasy of two people in some exquisite together state. It looks utterly heavenly, where nothing mundane, dull or ordinary comes in to interrupt, where all desires are satisfied, and dreams come true. But in real life, after the honeymoon stage, there is usually a sobering stage where the two people discover that alongside their loving feelings they have conflicting interests and needs. Also, they find that aspects of the other are irritating at best and drive them wild with exasperation or rage at worst. It is at this stage that some people throw in the towel. They leave because of their deep disappointment. Having idealised the other at the honeymoon stage, when 'real life' resumes the other person's imperfections loom too large in their mind. The lovely aspects of the person are eclipsed behind a fog of anger and resentment or start to fade to the status of not significant enough. Others stay in the relationship still believing that near perfection is a possibility. This drives them to attack anything about the other person that is less than perfect.

So why do some people get locked in a life of searching for the perfect mate when they don't exist?

The tormented quest of trying to get another person to take away the emptiness inside from years of unmet childhood emotional needs is actually very common. As couples expert Norwood (1986) says: 'When in our emptiness we go looking for love, we can only find emptiness'. Emotionally healthy relationships are based on reciprocity, as opposed to the one-way giving that is every infant's birthright. Thus, most people will fail to offer a perfect reparative, quasi re-parenting experience. For those who do offer this in an adult-to-adult relationship, with such complete devotion and servitude, the question is, what is happening to their own life, their own needs and their own creativity? Furthermore, when intense unmet infantile need is brought into a relationship, there is often all manner of clinging, demanding, emotional suffocation. Even despite the best intentions, this all too often drives the other person away.

Some people who have led such love-starved childhoods are stuck in time in a state of 'love made hungry'. They are so focused on not getting enough that they don't recognise what they are being given. They may believe that the love they are getting is only a pale shadow of the love other people are getting in their relationships (often idealised). This is particularly true of people who feel that their sibling got all the love or at least more than they did.

Sadly, some people get drawn into the other person's idealised fantasies, unaware of the screaming infant within. They end up believing that they are at fault for not managing to make this person totally happy. As one overgenerous, self-sacrificing man said of his embittered wife, 'I guess I just didn't delight and please her enough to draw her out of her depression. I should have tried harder. It was all my fault.'

There is double tragedy of course, when both people in a relationship are love-starved due to being emotionally neglected children. What can happen is that both people are looking for and hoping for emotional nourishment from the other. After a honeymoon period there is then often the terrible realisation that their partner is just as emotionally malnourished as themselves. Instead of their partner making up for all the love and comfort they never got as a child, they are shocked to find emotional neediness in that partner. This can leave them feeling deeply let down and in some cases repelled and contemptuous.

So what can be done?

Again, the exercises may help the participant to look at childhood origins of this endless search for the perfect partner. The exercises can heighten awareness of what the participant is getting rather than what he or she is *not* getting and so changing the cup from being half empty to half full. In terms of grieving childhood emptiness and childhood emotional deprivation, the exercises in the chapter called 'When love hurts' can be particularly useful here.

My relationship: Take off or stuck on the runway?

■Objective

This exercise is for people who are considering whether a key relationship in their life (with friend, partner or family member) has become too comfortable and safe, or whether, despite its limitations, with work, the relationship could still take off in some way. It will be a helpful exercise for someone who is actively considering whether to invest more in an important relationship, or perhaps leave and move on.

■Instructions to give the participant

When a relationship with friend, relative or partner feels more tiresome than rewarding, it can be hard to decide whether to keep working at it, just let it be as it is, or end it. Think of a relationship in your life that you feel ambivalent about in this way. Then look at the drawing of the aeroplane stuck on the runway. There are all manner of obstacles preventing the plane from taking off.

Write in the boxes (by the obstacles surrounding the plane) the things you think are preventing your relationship from really taking off (e.g. your lack of spontaneity when you are together, their lack of curiosity about or real interest in you and your life, rarely asked questions about how you are, your life). Then in the 'lovely things' box, write a list of the lovely things about this person and your relationship (e.g. the person's willingness to talk about the relationship/their sense of play and fun). From doing the exercise, it may become clear whether you think your relationship has a chance of 'taking off' at some time, so you will put the work in, or whether

the obstacles feel too many and too insurmountable. Alternatively, you may just lower your expectations and come to terms with the limitations.

■Development

If appropriate to the participant, discuss with them other relationships which offer the comfort of familiarity, yet are holding the person back from flourishing in important ways. It may be a relationship with a partner, friend, family member. If the participant thinks this is happening to them, ask them to draw a picture of what would happen if they were to give up the safe comfort of their relationship and leave or reduce together times. In the drawing, ask them to draw their fears and their hopes.

My relationship: Take off or stuck on the runway?

Obstacle

Obstacle

Obstacle

Obstacle

Obstacle

The lovely things box

Obstacle

Obstacle

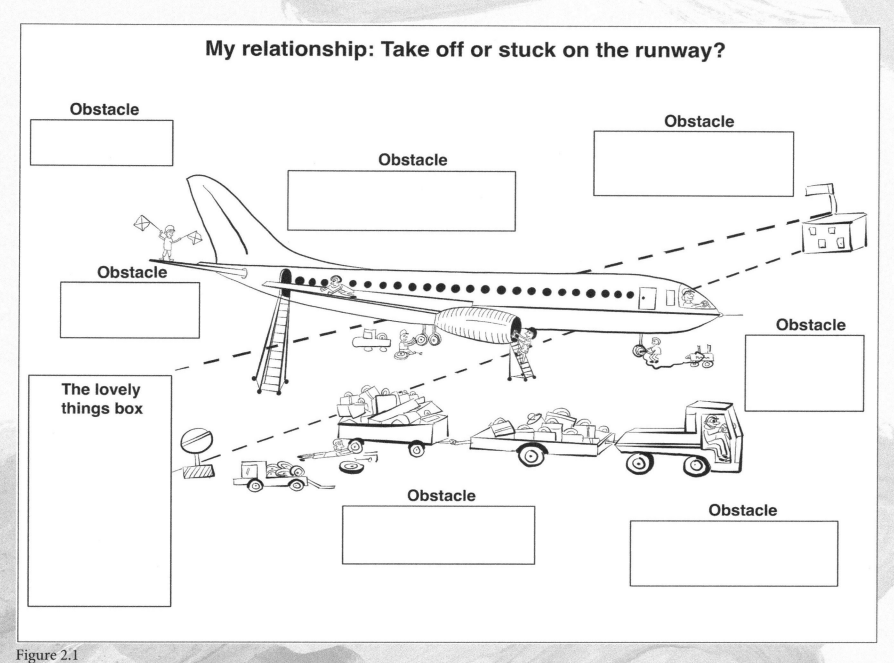

Figure 2.1

To leave or to stay?

■Objective

Sometimes it is hard to assess the quality of an important relationship in your life (with a friend, colleague, partner or family member). This being so, it can be difficult to decide how much time and energy to invest in it. One danger can be that of walking away from a fundamentally enriching relationship because it doesn't match up to a fairytale, idealised image you have of how close personal relationships should be. The other danger is staying in a relationship that doesn't really feed you in any way, just because it is safe and comfortable. So, in order to sharpen their thinking, this exercise is designed for participants to rehearse both the act of de-investing in an important relationship and the act of staying.

■Instructions to give the participant

Bring to mind a personal relationship (friend, partner, colleague, family member) you feel very ambivalent about.

Here are three film sets. On the set marked 'Film of your relationship now', draw or write all the images and feelings that come to mind when you think about this relationship. There is a list of feelings to the left of the picture to act as a prompt. On the set entitled 'Film of your life without this person in your life (painful version)', draw or write all the painful feelings/ images that come to mind when you think about your life if you decide to de-invest in the relationship from now on. Then on the set entitled 'Film of your life without this person in your life (hopeful version)', draw or write what you hope your life would look like, feel like if you decided to leave or de-invest in the relationship and so see them a lot less. (Again, there are prompt lists to help focus your mind.) Now stand back from the picture. What have you learnt about this person/relationship in your life as a result of the reflection time?

■Development

When my house burnt down I could see the rising sun.

(Anon)

This development will be helpful for the participant who is just staying in a relationship because it is safe and known, but ultimately deadening, or worse, actually destructive. Discuss with the participant the saying, 'When my house burnt down, I could see the rising sun'. Ask the participant if they can remember any times in their life when some awful event happened. Despite the shock and pain, it opened up something very creative or fulfilling that would not have occurred if the awful event hadn't occurred. If they have no such experiences, tell them about experiences of other people you know, or indeed of celebrity figures such as Tina Turner, who thrived once she left her abusive partner. Discuss how they could support themselves if they did dare to leave.

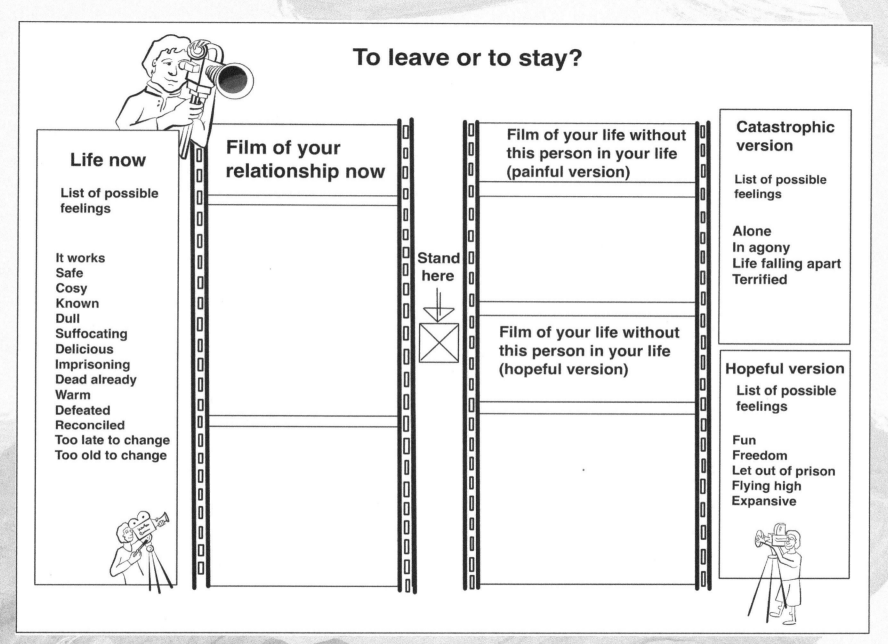

To leave or to stay?

Life now

List of possible feelings

It works
Safe
Cosy
Known
Dull
Suffocating
Delicious
Imprisoning
Dead already
Warm
Defeated
Reconciled
Too late to change
Too old to change

Film of your relationship now

Stand here

Film of your life without this person in your life (painful version)

Film of your life without this person in your life (hopeful version)

Catastrophic version

List of possible feelings

Alone
In agony
Life falling apart
Terrified

Hopeful version

List of possible feelings

Fun
Freedom
Let out of prison
Flying high
Expansive

Figure 2.2

The 'nothing much happening' times

■Objective

The aim of this exercise is for the participant to reflect on the quality of the key relationships in their life. By drawing on the images in the picture, the participant may develop a clearer sense in terms of which relationships in their life are enabling them to thrive and which are safe and comfortable, but ultimately leave their own emotional development at a standstill. The exploration of relationship with self is also key to this exercise.

■Instructions to give the participant

Do you ever feel like one of these figures in the picture, in the 'nothing much happening' times when you are alone or with others? In other words, in your relationship time with self (alone time) or with others, do you sometimes feel a kind of stuck, stagnant or dried-up energy, or is it actually a needed 'down time' drifting, chill-out time in a too-busy life. Write on one or more of the positive bubbles what you feel are the good things about the 'nothing much happening' times and on the negative bubbles what you feel are the bad things about such times.

If it seems you have more negative feelings about these times, what or who in your life might bring you the jolt, motivation or emotional strength to help you shift out of these ways of being with self or others, if instead of useful down time they feel stuck, stagnant and not good for your mental health?

■Development – Relationship aliveness/ dullness review

When people are unsure whether key relationships in their life are emotionally nourishing or not, the 'Relationship aliveness/dullness review' (see Table 2.1) can be particularly useful. It can help a participant to become clearer as to whether or not they want to keep investing emotionally in a certain relationship in their life. It can challenge them to consider whether they are settling for comfort and safety instead of seeking relationships that are enlivening, nourishing and personally developing. Ask the participant to think back over an appropriate timescale of their choice about a key relationship. Then tick which of the following relationship events, if any, happened between them and the other person. The participant can then speak about what they have learnt about the quality of this relationship.

Table 2.1

Relationship aliveness/dullness review	Yes	No
You told them about an important feeling, e.g. a desire, a hope, a longing, and they listened with real interest and understanding.		
They told you about an important feeling, e.g. a desire, a hope, a longing, and you listened with real interest and understanding.		
You told them something you appreciated about them or appreciated them doing for you or something they were good at.		
They told you something they appreciated about you, or something you had done or something you were good at.		
You both engaged in playful banter of some sort or shared laughter.		
You did something new together or talked about an adventure/new experience you intend to share in the near future.		
You shared a lovely time together.		
A hello or goodbye was a real moment of connection or you had a really warm exchange.		
You asked each other for help with a concern, problem or worry.		
You were spontaneously physically affectionate towards each other.		

The nothing much happening times

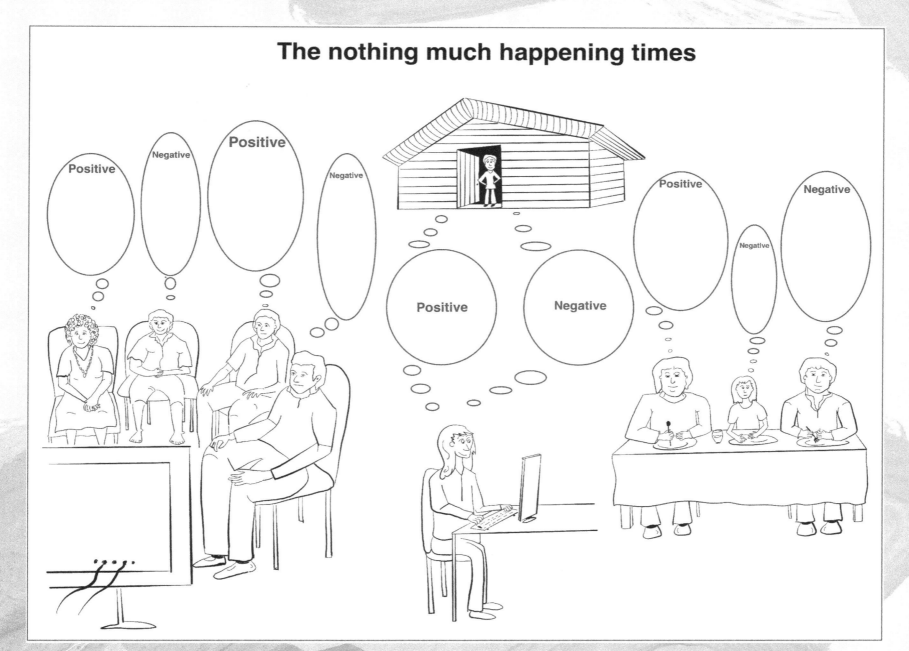

Figure 2.3

A relationship that's holding me back

■Objective

Not only is life enriched through shared quality time with another person, but it also enhances personal development. Due to an ongoing lack of positive social interaction in their lives, some people are developmentally arrested at a far younger age than their chronological age (Perry, 2002). This exercise is for people who think that a key relationship in their life, is holding them back in some way, preventing them from developing and thriving.

■Instructions to give the participant

Think of a relationship which is central to your life (family, friend, partner, work colleague) and yet one you are concerned is holding you back in some way, squashing your life force or creativity, perhaps, or badly affecting your ability to use life well. Then take a look at the picture. When you think of this person/relationship in your life, do you ever feel like a figure in any of these pictures? If so, tick them or colour them in. You can also include your *relationship to life in general* as one of your relationships!
  You may also like to add:

Sometimes = S
Often = O
Frequently = F
Always = A

If none of these images seems to fit what you feel in terms of the particular frustrations you have with this relationship, draw your own images

somewhere on the picture. Now rehearse breaking free by getting in the hot air balloon. Write in the appropriate balloons: your worst fears and best hopes.

■Development – Leap in the dark

This exercise is for participants who believe that a significant relationship in their life is preventing them from really thriving. Ask the participant to draw a picture called 'Leap in the dark'. In the picture, ask them to draw themselves leaping away from their relationship and landing in an imaginary land in which people (fictitious or real) are encouraging, inspiring, extremely supportive. Ask the participant to draw these people (stick figures will do) and then give each person a speech bubble. What are they saying? What does the participant want to do on an imaginary day out with these people? Discuss with the participant what support they need to dare to taste life anew, to take a risk, to live a larger life, to stop depriving themselves from enjoying 'the nicest possibilities in their short lives' (Zinker, 1978).

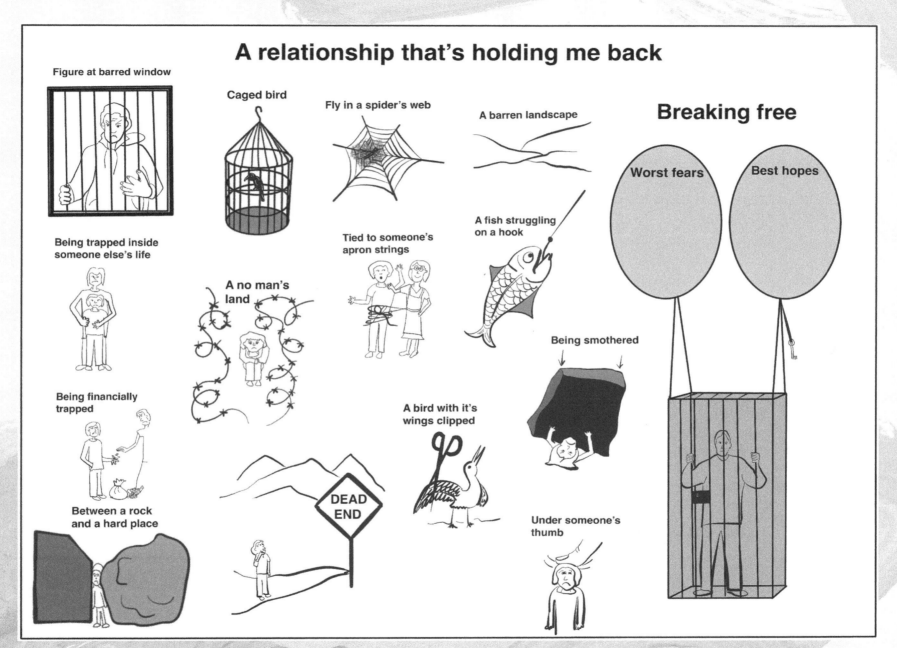

A relationship that's holding me back

Figure at barred window

Caged bird

Fly in a spider's web

A barren landscape

Breaking free

Worst fears

Best hopes

Being trapped inside someone else's life

A no man's land

Tied to someone's apron strings

A fish struggling on a hook

Being financially trapped

Being smothered

A bird with it's wings clipped

Between a rock and a hard place

DEAD END

Under someone's thumb

Figure 2.4

People who energise. People who drain

■Objective

This exercise is designed for the participant to consider the quality of their relationship life, with the aim of trying to cut down on time spent with people who are emotionally draining and more time with people who energise them. This is such an important contributing factor to quality of life.

■Instructions to give the participant

Think of people in your life whom you find or have found emotionally draining. These are people with whom you feel tired or somewhat empty or alone during or after spending time with them. Then think of the people in your life (past and present) who make you feel alive, expansive and fulfilled. (The latter can be teachers/mentors/therapists, past or present, as well as people in your personal life.)

Look at the pictures. If you feel that someone in your life is represented by a particular drawing/symbol, write their name underneath. Choose one of the energies even if they are like this some of the time, not all of the time. The same name may appear on more than one symbol. Now stand back and look at what you have drawn.

How might you change the amount of time you spend with the people who drain you? Or how might you speak to them about the effect they have on you? Sometimes people are simply not aware of their difficult energy and are very willing to change for the better with constructive feedback. How might you spend more time with people who energise you? Or if they are no longer in your life, how might you bring these people to mind more as each time you do, it will also nourish you?

■Development – Self as energy sapper

Of course, it is possible to find yourself draining as well as feeling drained by others. For example, constant self-put-downs and negative self-talk can leave you feeling utterly low and miserable, e.g. 'You are stupid/lazy/a time-waster', 'Look, you've done it again, the same mistake again!', etc. Ask the participant to do the same exercise, but this time on a new piece of paper, drawing some of their own draining energies (e.g. their depressed self-state, agitated self-state, etc.). Ask them also to draw their self-states that feel energising and uplifting. Ask them to give each energy state a title (e.g. 'defeated drone' or 'confident flow').

Discuss with them how they could be more supportive to themselves when they are experiencing one of their draining energies. What do they need to do? Who do they need to be with? If negative self-talk is draining them, it can help to write down some self-supportive statements that they can then play in their mind. So, for example, in response to a 'lazy slob' critical self-talk, they can say something like, 'It's very important for you to have a rest. With a 'pull yourself together' critical self-talk, they can say something like, 'It's understandable that with all this going on for you in your life at the moment you are feeling down. How about calling X or Y?' Many lovely energy states are pretty much people-dependent, meaning it's hard to access them without being around the right sort of people. So ask the participant who they need to be around more? Then ask them what general changes they may need to make to their life in order to decrease the amount of time they spend in their draining emotional energy states.

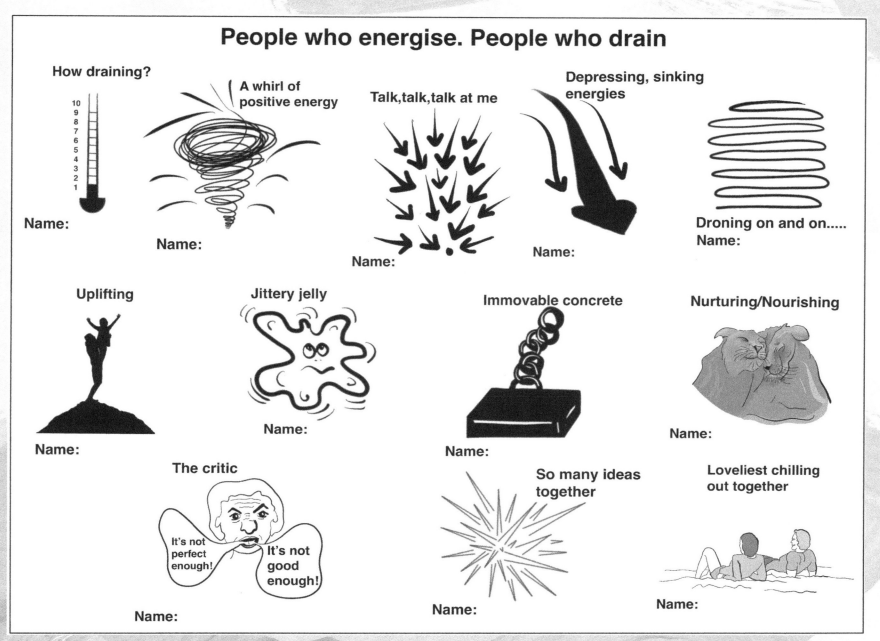

People who energise. People who drain

Figure 2.5

Too many takers and not enough givers

■Objective

This exercise is designed to reflect on all the people in your life who have needs of you and to see how you can rebalance your life with more giving and less taking, including how to give more to yourself if those around you are not capable of doing so (e.g. because they are children, or incapacitated in some way).

■Instructions to give the participant

Look at this picture. Write on the 'taking' white lines all the people in your life who need from you in some way. It is not meant to be blaming of them – many will have a right to need things from you (e.g. your children, people at work, elderly parent). Then write on the table what you would like to be given more of in your life. This should include what you would like to give more of to yourself (e.g. alone time, spa days, acknowledgement for what you do give).

When you have finished, stand back and look at what you have drawn. What do you feel about your life as you survey the scene? In the face of all the demands on you, what could you do to bring more emotional richness into your life to nourish you? Are there any people who have needs of you that you could give less to/put some boundaries down? For example, 'I have been thinking. What I need for me is to give to you in this way, but I no longer want to do x or y for you, because . . .'

Are you appreciating enough the people in your life who do give you things? When did you last express gratitude to them?

■Development – The place of not enough and the place of more than enough

This exercise in sandplay takes the idea of abundance and depletion into a wider arena in terms of a review of the participant's life as a whole. If you need more information on this technique, see 'About sandplay and how to use it' at the beginning of this book.

1 Divide the sandplay box into two. One side will be called the 'Place of not enough' and the other side the 'Place of more than enough'. Place objects in each side of the tray to accurately describe the different aspects of your life. What do you feel satisfied with in your life and what are the deficits and the losses?

2 Once you've done this, find a miniature object to be you and place yourself in this 'Place of more than enough'. What do you feel being there? What would you do if you spent a day in this place?

3 Then place yourself in the 'Place of not enough'. What do you feel being there? What would you do if you spent a day in this place?

4 Now make up and enact a story about how your miniature object can get from the 'Place of not enough' to the 'Place of more than enough'. Allow yourself to move into the realm of fantasy and the absurd. Don't think too much of reality or logic!

5 Although you may have created a story that uses all manner of magical powers, there is often a grain of truth in such metaphorical exploration. What would this be for your life? If you can't think of this now, it may occur to you once you have let the image live on in your mind for a while.

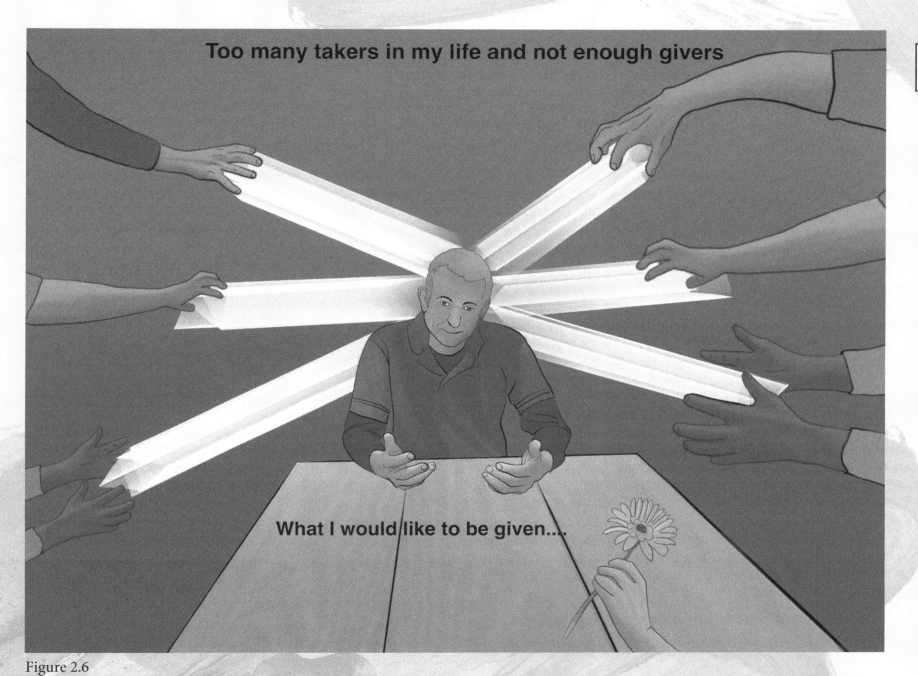

Figure 2.6

Am I expecting too much from her/him?

■Objective

This exercise is for people to consider whether they are unreasonably expecting too much from someone in their life or are in an emotionally depriving relationship, as sometimes it's hard to tell the difference. The former is a common problem: a person has emotional needs that were never adequately met in childhood. Then in later life, often without being aware of it, they put pressure on intimates to satisfy all those unmet childhood needs (e.g. to be adored, to be listened to endlessly, to be repeatedly soothed and calmed). In this sense, they want the other person to act towards them as the adoring, all-giving parent they never had. The problem with this is that parent – child relationships are indeed one-way, whilst emotionally healthy relationships must be based on reciprocity.

■Instructions to give the participant

Sometimes it can be unclear as to whether an important relationship is nourishing or not. It can be difficult to know whether you have unreasonable expectations fuelled by unmet needs from childhood, or whether you are putting up with emotional deprivation in this relationship because of low self-esteem or fear of aloneness. Or perhaps you've never had a truly emotionally nourishing relationship, so you don't know what is possible or what emotional nourishment really feels like.

In order to become clearer about the quality and potential of your relationship, fill in the checklists below. If a category on either of the lists is not relevant to your relationship, just leave it blank.

If you've ticked the 'Yes' box for a lot of the statements in the 'Emotionally depriving relationship checklist' and the 'No' box for lots of statements in the 'Emotionally nourishing relationship checklist', you are indeed in an emotionally depriving relationship. Then it will be important to ask yourself, 'What makes me stay?' Think of your childhood relationships. How might you be replaying emotionally depriving relationships from your past in your present? What could you do about it, by either trying to change the culture of this relationship or spending more time with people who are rich in emotional supplies, so to speak? If, however, you ticked a lot of 'No' boxes in the first table and a lot of 'Yes' boxes in the second table, consider how your unmet childhood needs may be putting undue pressure on your relationship. Think of going into personal counselling or therapy for a period, where these needs can be addressed and worked through appropriately, so you don't spoil your relationship.

Table 2.2

Emotionally depriving relationship checklist		
Tick which of these are regular features in your relationship. Does the other person often:	Yes	No
Forget important days, e.g. your birthday, anniversary?		
Blow hot and cold, i.e. is really loving one minute, then cold or hostile the next?		
Fail to say what he/she really appreciates about you?		
Give you cold or indifferent greetings or partings?		
Show more interest in their phone, television, computer, newspaper, etc. than in you?		
Punish you with such things as cold silences, guilt-tripping, being a martyr, passive aggression, put-downs, criticism or explosive outbursts?		
Nag or criticise you far more times than appreciate you? *(for emotional health, people need on average six appreciations for each criticism)*		
Frequently fail to listen to what interests you?		

Table 2.2 (Continued)

Emotionally depriving relationship checklist		
Tick which of these are regular features in your relationship. Does the other person often:	**Yes**	**No**
Provide little or no spontaneous physical affection?		
Fail to go out of their way to do something for you?		
Raise your expectations and then disappoint you by not fulfilling what they said?		
In arguments move into blame, not resolution?		
Diminish or not appreciate your gestures of goodwill, compliments, generosity, love, gifts?		
Radiate gloom?		
Deliver below-the-belt attacks?		
Threaten to leave?		
Make odious comparisons between you and other people?		
Offer you dull/superficial and/or hostile contact for much of the time, yet is alive/interested/playful/humorous with other people?		
Publicly ridicule you?		

Table 2.3

Emotionally nourishing relationship checklist		
With this person are there frequent times when:	**Yes**	**No**
You feel appreciated by them?		
You feel listened to by them?		
They treat you with real respect?		
They are genuinely interested in how you are, asking and listening to what you are feeling or something that has happened to you?		
They go out of their way to do something kind for you?		
They are genuinely pleased to see you?		
They say goodbye to you in a warm, demonstrative way?		
You feel really liked by them and valued by them?		
They are playful with you?		

■Development – Saying 'no' to relationship poverty and seeking out relational plenty

If the participant realises from these checklists that they are putting up with a bad deal relationship, ask them to explore the following question: What negative self-talk in your head holds you back from challenging this person, or, if appropriate, leaving this relationship and seeking out relational plenty? If the participant struggles to answer, give them a list of common reasons why people put up with depriving relationships and in so doing blight their lives:

- I would never manage on my own.
- I don't think I could do better.
- No one else would want me.
- If only I keep on loving them, my love will heal them eventually.
- But sometimes they are nice to me (seeing rarities as pearls).
- It's not that bad.
- I don't really deserve to be treated better.

The following quotation can also be a good discussion point:

> But when they give a history of the relationship, one wonders at their blindness. Their choice [of partner] seems pathological or perverse. There had been indications that the other was incapable of reciprocating, or loving, or accepting them in the way they desire. They had been pursuing an alluring but rejecting [person], exciting yet frustrating. This other person initially may have offered conditions of hope, but it fails to satisfy. It has awakened an intensity of yearning, but is essentially the elusive object of desire, seemingly there but just out of reach.
>
> (Armstrong-Perlman, 1991)

Disappointing relationship or futile quest for perfect mate?

■Objective

This exercise is designed for people who feel disappointed in their choice of friend or partner to stand back for a while and try to sort out whether they are locked in a futile search for a perfect mate (there are none). In so doing they are not appreciating what they *have* in their relationship, or whether there is a reality of 'not a great fit' between the two of them and of having too little in common.

■Instructions to give the participant

If you are in a relationship with someone which feels somewhat disappointing, this exercise is designed for you to consider whether this is based on your belief of some amazing partner out there who doesn't ever exist (and in so doing underappreciate the riches you do have between you) or whether you really are very different and so it would be wise to find someone with whom you have more in common.

Many people search in vain, year after year, for that someone special. Some people however, are looking for a person who doesn't actually exist in reality. Rather it is an idealised version of a human being, and no one is one! We all have flaws, faults, blind spots, really annoying habits, etc. Yet some people have such high hopes that if they just keep looking they will find that particular person who will transport them into a bright new world of undying love, blissful merger, or whatever is the person's fairy-tale dream. People locked in hope for the idealised other in this way are destined for a life of disappointment and unfulfilled yearnings. Tragically, some people end up spoiling or destroying much of what they do have in the relationship by constant criticism of their partner's imperfections, a process beautifully described by Julia Segal: 'They continually compare real life with some mythical kind of perfect love, perfect understanding, perfect bliss, and they turn their considerable powers to destroying anything that fails to match up' (Segal, 1985).

Write in the picture your unspoken or spoken disappointments and fears about your relationship and then write down what you imagine your partner's disappointments, fears and doubts are. If you are in a same-sex relationship just change the people drawings if you like. Then write in the 'What is good' box the good things about your relationship. Then stand back and look at the picture. Do you think you are underappreciating the good things between you or are you really incompatible, or feel that you cannot flourish in life if you stay in this relationship?

■Development

If the participant has found the idea that they may be in a futile quest for the perfect mate, they may be interested in knowing some of the common child-hood origins when people leave relationships time after time due to feelings of disappointment. This is usually to do with chronically unmet emotional needs in childhood. From this, there can be born a belief (often totally out of conscious awareness) that the other person is supposed to give them everything they never got as a child, such as undying, totally unconditional love and devotion or engaged, excited adventure time after time. They may bring all manner of unmet infantile needs into their relationship with the expectation and anticipation that the other person would somehow meet them. When the latter fails to be the ever-flowing breast, so to speak, there can be a sense of betrayal and bitterness. Underlying feelings are usually not voiced: 'I feel deeply disappointed in you. I had this dream of us, you see, that you would be a fairytale princess/ prince and make up for all my childhood years of deprivation and hurt, that you'd be my perfect caretaker.' This would, of course, be far more palatable to hear than the usual recriminations: 'You're so selfish and mean. Self, self, self!' 'You're never really there for me, you're married to your job, your computer.'

Figure 2.7

Life-changing relationships

■Essential theory

And if by chance we find each other, it's beautiful. If not, it can't be helped.
(Perls, 1969)

We can only develop socially and emotionally by being in meaningful relationships with other people. We cannot develop by being on our own, watching television, using a computer, texting or emailing. If we don't get enough enriching face to face relational experiences, then parts of the self will remain undrawn, undeveloped and not fully realised. Furthermore, positive relationships are key for mental, physical health and actual brain development (Ybarra et al., 2008; Johnson et al., 2016; Teo, 2015).

If we are lucky, we will meet people in our lives who will ignite our creativity, spontaneity, passion, enthusiasm for life and all it has to offer and enable us to fulfil our human potential. Such connections often happen in intimate relationships but not necessarily so. Some long-term intimate relationships have become so 'comfortable' that the two people have not had many moments of real meeting in years. On the other hand, we can be changed by moments of strong emotional connection with someone whom we have only known for a short period of time.

True moments of meeting, when you feel deeply connected to another person, can change you forever. As Polster (1987) states: 'When you are in full contact [with someone], change is inevitable'. In moments of meeting there are no closed doors, no restrictions to the flow of things. Any shyness or awkwardness is entirely eclipsed by the strength of the emotional charge between you. This is depicted beautifully in the following quotation:

At our first meeting, we talked with continually increasing intimacy. We seemed to sink through layer after layer of what was superficial, till gradually both reached the central fire. It was an experience unlike any other that I have known. We looked into each other's eyes, half appalled and half intoxicated to find ourselves together in such a region. The emotion was as intense and passionate as love, and at the same time all-embracing. I came away bewildered, and hardly able to find my way among ordinary affairs.

(Yalom, 1980)

■What qualifies as a transformational moment of meeting?

- Something just clicks, and the conversation flows with such ease; it feels as if it could go on and on without stopping.
- You are aware that you have entered an intensely rich vista of human relating.
- The encounter may take you into previously uncharted ways of being and emotional energy states. You feel intensely alive.
- You feel really seen, met, understood or engaged with.
- 'To the extent one truly "turns towards the other" one is altered. To the extent one brings the other to life, one also becomes more fully alive.'

(Yalom, 1980)

■The transformational power of loving relationships and the chemistry of love

Any book on relationships would not be complete without talking about love, and in the context of this chapter, the transformational power of loving someone in peace (as opposed to in torment). In other parts of the book we consider the inevitable pain and suffering caused by lost love, or loss of a loved one. But here we will concentrate on the ways in which a deeply loving relationship can transform someone's life and enrich it in the most amazing ways. When we love deeply, we are also intensely alive. The reverse is also true. If we cannot fully love, life cannot be lived to the full.

Whilst love is a difficult concept to speak about in brain terms, it is becoming increasingly clear to scientists that it strongly activates a symphony of positive arousal brain chemicals, including three very important ones, namely oxytocin, opioids and prolactin. In neuroscience it is these chemicals that have come to be known as the key bonding chemistries. Opioids, oxytocin and prolactin optimally activated in combination can make you feel that everything is well in your world, with thoughts and feelings taking you to a very warm place inside your head. Opioids and oxytocin are also powerful anti-aggressive anti-anxiety chemicals. They can dramatically diminish negative feelings, especially feelings of loneliness, isolation and worry. Neuroscientists also think that the finest human qualities of generosity, kindness, compassion and expansiveness towards others are opioid-based. What is more, scientists have found that psychological strength is 'opioid-mediated'. In other words, during those times when opioids are optimally activated in our brains, we are far more likely to enjoy social confidence, the capacity to think well, and be able to calm ourselves down quickly under stress. All in all, optimally activated opioids and oxytocin (in combination with other key chemicals) form a vital foundational system for emotional health (Panksepp and Biven, 2012).

In terms of relationships, research shows that mammals (both humans and animals) prefer to spend more time in the presence of those who frequently enjoy a strong activation of opioids and oxytocin in their brains. We also treasure those people in our lives who strongly activate opioids in our brains, because they are so warm with a real capacity for calm. They make the sun shine. They take our stress away. As love (and feeling loved) is opioid-based, it means we are nicer to be around and so we are likely to receive a far more positive response from the world.

■Love is more than just a joy juice in your brain

Of course, love is more than just a joy juice in your brain, more than just a particular chemical activation. In other words, when we love, our thoughts, perceptions, feelings and actions are all being affected by those brain chemicals described above, but at the same time, our states of mind are affecting our brain chemistry. In other words, we must remember that there is mind as well as brain, and the immensely complex interrelationship and energetic flow between the two.

■Our genetically programmed need for strong emotional bonds

The need for strong emotional bonds can be mistakenly seen as clinging, over-dependency, or regressive infantile need. This is totally wrong. In terms of the CARE system in the limbic part of our brain (Panksepp and Biven, 2012), whether we like it or not, we are all genetically programmed to need close emotional bonds. We can try to override this, but the price in terms of emotional and physical ill health is high. Loneliness and isolation are as bad for your health as smoking 15 cigarettes a day (Holt-Lunstad et al., 2015).

Some people mistakenly think that bonding behaviour is something belonging to childhood. This is wrong. It continues throughout life. However, we develop strong emotional bonds towards just a few people, usually in a clear hierarchy in terms of strength of bond (or if you like strength of opioid activation). We can like many people, be very fond of them, but we will develop strong emotional bonds to just a few. That is how the CARE system in the limbic part of our brain operates (Panksepp and Biven, 2012). So, when people say, 'I love everybody' or 'I love everybody in this group', this is a sugar-sweet, scientific inaccuracy.

■No rose-coloured spectacles

Just because we love some people in our lives, it does not of course mean that we will always feel loving towards them. Life's stressors, anxieties and anger impinge, and when they do, the release of opioids and oxytocin are blocked in the brain and cascades of stress chemicals become dominant instead. However, for those people whose neurological CARE system (Panksepp and Biven, 2012) – their attachment system – is functioning optimally, opioids will trigger once again after appropriate emotional regulation (from self or asking for help to regulate from others). This means that the person is far less likely to 'sweat the small stuff' and be far more likely to be stable under stress. In contrast, people who 'love in torment', meaning loving as a rollercoaster of excitement, hurt, fear, rage, etc., will find it difficult to come down from toxic stress to tolerable stress and then to feeling loving feelings again. We can see this in people who hold grudges, stay with resentments and develop real hatred for a long time.

■Childhood origins of loving in peace

The ability to form deeply fulfilling loving relationships is often established very early in life. Consistent loving moments of meeting between child and parent during the first years of life, through face-to-face interactions, empathy, attunement and play (all stress-reducing interactions, not stress-inducing), will establish vitally important systems in the brain (CARE, SEEKING and PLAY), optimising the activation of opioids and oxytocin (Sunderland, 2016).

Loving in peace means that a child feels very safe in their parents' love. This is because that love is a consistent love, not an on–off love. In other words, it is a love that will not suddenly move into coldness, indifference, shame or contempt. As part of this, the parent will discipline the child in ways that give them clear boundaries, but do not frighten them, as fear can all too easily kill off love. The parental love will also be a non-needy love, a non-suffocating love, one that does not overwhelm the child with the parents' unmet emotional needs. It is also an unconditional love, as opposed to a love conditional on achievement, total compliance, behaving in certain ways, or on not having certain feelings such as rage or jealousy. It is a love based on the fact that the parent is able to meet the child deeply, whether in pain or in joy. The child will also be confident that their parent will meet their spontaneous expressions of love with grace, rather than with shame, indifference or dismissal. Attachment theory is key to all this. Secure attachment means the child is secure that their parent will be consistently emotionally responsive. As John Bowlby, the originator of attachment theory, said:

> So deeply established are his expectations [of an emotionally responsive parent] and so repeatedly have they been confirmed that, as an adult, he finds it difficult to imagine any other kind of world. This gives him an almost unconscious assurance that whenever and wherever he might be in difficulty, there are always trustworthy figures available that will come to his aid. He will therefore approach the world with confidence and when faced with potentially alarming situations, is likely to tackle them effectively or to seek help in doing so.

(Bowlby, 1973)

It is clear from the above that the child's love for a parent is not automatic. Just as we cannot command the clouds to move so the sun will shine, parents cannot command love from their child.

That said, if love has gone wrong in early life, effective counselling or psychotherapy can enable a person to love in peace or dare to love again.

People you've been flying with

They keep taking each other to the sun,
They find they can easily.
(Ted Hughes, in Keegan, 1993)

■Objective

Some people we meet transform our lives. We are never the same again, as the saying goes, 'I am the people I have known'. These are people who bring out the best in us, who empower us, who enable the denied, neglected aspects of the self to surface and flourish. For some people this may mean the birth of a new confidence; for others it may mean the birth of a more expansive self, a more fun self or a more creative self. All this could never be achieved on one's own.

Bruce Perry (2002) rightly names what these splendid people bring us as 'the gift that keeps on giving'. He means that even if the person leaves or dies, the experience of knowing them continues to enrich us. Memories of such people need to be treasured, savoured and frequently brought to mind: hence the purpose of this exercise.

This can be a particularly powerful exercise, which may move the participant to tears. This is because we often suppress positive feelings just as frequently as we suppress negative feelings. Sometimes we deny or are cut off from strong feelings of gratitude, joy, love and exhilaration because we need someone to help us bear the intensity of these feelings. Hopefully, this exercise will provide participants with a safe enough arena to do just that.

■Instructions to give the participant

Think of people in your past or present who have changed your life, enabled you to use life well in important and significant ways. Melanie Klein, a famous psychoanalyst referred to these people as 'our inner wealth'. If you have known several of these people, you are, metaphorically speaking, a millionaire.

The memories of such people are like treasures. If you keep these treasures buried in your mind, or if you try to cut off from their emotional charge, they lose their power. If, on the other hand, you imbue them with fresh energy by bringing them to mind, by speaking about them with someone who can listen well and appreciate their importance, they can become far more of a life-enhancing resource.

On the picture, write the names of the people in your life with whom you have been flying. Then fill in 'The place they took me to' by writing words for or drawing the psychological place they brought into your life, e.g. a kindly world, a world of fun, a land of inspiration and opportunity, a place of 'Let's'. It doesn't matter if the person is dead or the relationship has ended because once you have been flying with someone in this way you are changed forever. What do you feel and what are you thinking when you look at what you have drawn or written?

■Development – Gratitude notes

Unexpressed gratitude makes us poorer. In this 'unfinished sentence' exercise, ask the participant to think of one or more people who have changed their life for the better. Ask them to finish the following sentences (repeat for each different person):

- I remember when you . . .
- I like/d it when we . . .

- I love/d it when we . . .
- Thank you for encouraging me with . . .
- I am so grateful to you for . . .
- The greatest gift you have left me is . . .

If the person is still alive, it may be appropriate to support the participant to say these things directly to the person.

People you've been flying with

The place they took me to:

The place they took me to:

The place they took me to:

The place they took me to:

The place they took me to:

Figure 3.1

Flying together as a group

When people feel profoundly connected . . . this kind of relationship is so important to the soul that many have said there is nothing more precious in life.

(Moore, 1994a)

■Objective

When groups are functioning well they have an energetic force that is just not possible for only one single person. The combined energies of the particular personalities can result in the most amazing creativity and productivity. This is not age-dependent. A group of eight-year-olds can build an incredible den, a group of six-year-olds can make a wonderful sand world on the beach, and a group of emotionally charged adults can turn an original business idea into a roaring success. Yet all too often we fall into a rut of doing things solo or just as part of a twosome. So this exercise focuses on the participant's most memorable times of exciting and pleasurable group experiences. These memories of being an integral part of a group's creative force are important to bring to mind as a way of imbuing them with energy. It is hoped that this will then motivate the participant to actively seek out ways of being part of more such positive group experiences in their life. The exercise also includes looking at negative group experiences so that these can be more carefully avoided in future.

■Instructions to give the participant

Think of times in your life when you were part of a group whose creative energy was exhilarating. When part of that group, you were flying high. For each group experience you can remember, name the event or group on these various flying carpets. Then fill in the core beliefs about yourself or other people that may have resulted from these powerful experiences, e.g.

'I can be creative/fun/powerful'. If most of these important group experiences happened in childhood or adolescence and you have not had any or too few such experiences in adulthood, how could you be more proactive? What do you need to do in your life to ensure that you let more exhilarating group experiences into your life?

Just as some groups have the potential to be highly creative, others can of course be destructive and psychologically damaging. So turn to the pictures in the section called 'Being part of a dysfunctional group' and think of negative group experiences in your life at home, at work or in other contexts. Label the memories that come to mind. (For some people these will be in their original family.) Then, as before, write the negative core beliefs you think you developed as a result of these experiences.

Emotional energy is so contagious that one person in a group with a critical or gloomy energy can bring down the whole group. What do you need to do in your life to ensure that you don't repeat more negative group experiences like the ones you have indicated here?

■Development – Family groups

Ask the participant to draw their family group as animals or plants or buildings. When they have done this, ask them to comment on what they have drawn, the positioning, the size and shape of the family members. Then ask them to write or draw the key events when the group was flying high or full of gloom. Ask the participant what they have learnt from these family experiences, for better or worse, about being in groups. How have these family group experiences affected the participant's motivation to be part of other groups today?

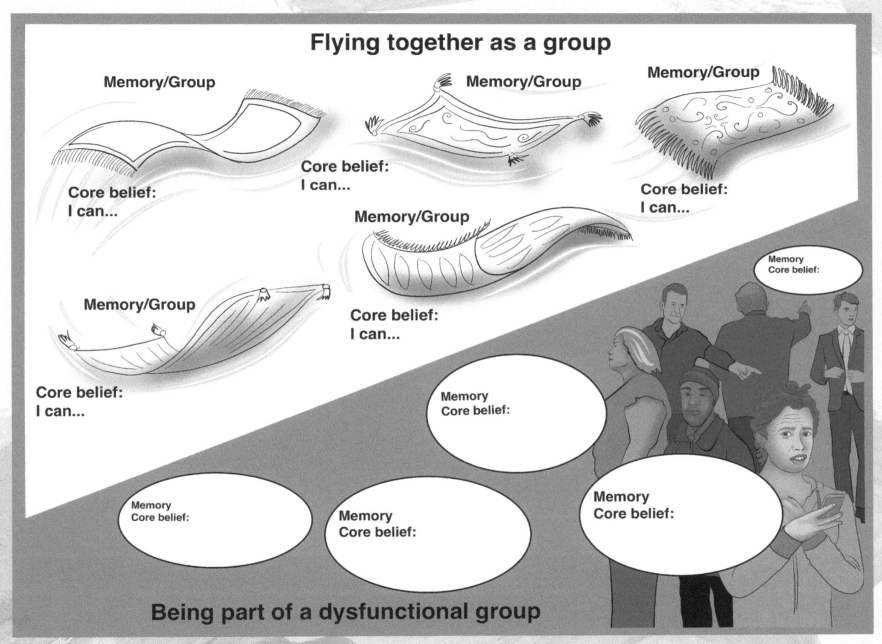

Figure 3.2

Collecting moments, not things

The quality of contact determines whether life 'passes by' or whether it is lived to the full.

(Clarkson, 1989)

■Objective

Moments of emotionally charged positive connection with another person can be transformative. A key researcher called Daniel Stern found that such moments of meeting last about ten seconds. Within that time, both people are perfectly attuned to each other, both are riding the same feeling contour, as if on the same surfboard (Stern, 2004). Moments of meeting strongly activate positive arousal chemicals in the brain (optimal levels of noradrenalin, dopamine and opioids) in the brain, as a result of which a long-term memory will be laid down. You will never forgot them!

This exercise is about bringing these moments of meeting to mind, sharing them, celebrating them, savouring them. When remembered in this way, the life-enriching properties of these moments can become better integrated into self-worth and the sense of emotional well-being.

■Instructions to give the participant

Think of the emotionally charged positive encounters and moments of meeting you have had with another person that you will never forget because they were life-enhancing in some way. In one such moment you may have felt intensely sad and yet profoundly moved because someone was comforting you. In another you may have felt intensely loving. In others you may have felt deeply understood by something someone said. But whatever you were feeling, it is the quality of contact with the other person that made these moments so significant. The other person was so connected with you in your sadness, your laughter, your exhilaration, and you *knew* they were. It is these moments of meeting that are crucial to the development of us as persons.

We can also have powerful moments on our own when connecting in a profound way to a place, or to a beautiful view or to a feeling of peace inside ourselves. Again, there is an unforgettable feeling of 'All is well in the world'.

Look at the picture. In the circle entitled 'With someone', draw or write the moments of meeting you remember. These moments can be with the same or different people. In the circle entitled 'On your own', draw or write the moments of intense calm, peace, fulfilment, etc. that you remember having on your own.

Then if you feel able speak about these moments, (at the level you feel comfortable) to take them from the private realm to the public witness of the listener, and in so doing imbuing them with the attention and energy they so richly deserve. These 'life gems' are too important to remain either private or dormant in your mind.

■Development – Oh, how we laugh!

See next page.

Collecting moments not things

On your own

With someone

Figure 3.3

Oh, how we laugh!

■Objective

Some of the most intimate moments between two human beings involve laughing together. You have to feel really secure in the presence of someone to do that, knowing they won't shame you or criticise you in any way. In fact, from animal psychology we know that when there is any fear around, all play and all humour stops. In the famous cat fur experiment, when a tuft of cat fur was placed near to some rats who were playing, the rat play ceased totally. The animals continued to stop playing for up to five successive days – even when the cat had been taken away! This is how powerful our brain's FEAR system is in blocking our brain's PLAY system (Panksepp, 2001). Times of shared humour can be some of our most treasured memories and so need to be re-visited and told to an attentive listener who can share in, endorse and appreciate the delight.

■Instructions to give the participant

Sharing humour is a form of exquisite playing together and laughing together means that the quality of safety in the relationship is pretty high. Such moments need to be treasured and shared rather than just stored away in one's memory, never to see the light of day, so to speak. So in this exercise, write down some of your most treasured funny moments. Think how they brought intimacy between you and the other person or people at that moment. Then tell them again now. Play in the form of humour triggered the loveliest brain chemicals, namely opioids and dopamine, which are so vital for mental and physical health.

■Development

If this has been really powerful for the participant repeat the exercise, but this time share treasured moments of shared awe, shared group triumph and shared best days together.

Oh, how we laugh!

List of treasured funny moments

-
-
-
-
-
-
-

Figure 3.4

Knights (posing as people)

■Objective

In theory our parents will support us, soothe us, help us with all the many challenging situations we encounter, as children and as teenagers, and encourage us in endless ways; then send us into the world ready to take on anything. But for many people it doesn't quite happen like that and the people who do support and encourage us in quite extraordinary ways are not, in fact, our parents but other people. They are what I call 'Knights'. Knights develop us in profound ways. They may enable us to feel fully for the first time. They may enable us to feel true compassion for the first time. They may enable us to know joy for the first time, or to love in peace for the first time. Whatever they have enabled in us, their support has been breathtakingly moving.

Such people must be talked about with a listening other as the 'first public' (Ross, 1992) to such profound life events. Moreover, to share with a listening other the knights we have known can really strengthen the positive presence of these people in our minds. So this exercise is about helping participants to celebrate these positive figures in their life. Reminiscence is key. Allow listening time to hear any funny, fond, poignant memories they have of being with these life-changing people.

> *Knights are the stuff of myth and fairy tale,*
> *But there are some knights on earth, who look like ordinary people.*
> *Knights are fearless in fighting for fairness.*
> *Knights take you by the hand and don't let go.*
> *Knights will be with you along the way,*
> *Until you feel safe again.*
> (The author, from the book *Monica Plum's Horrid Problem*)

■Instructions to give the participants

If you have known one Knight (posing as a person) in your life you are lucky. If you have known several you are truly fortunate indeed. Think about the people in your life who have been supportive to you in quite incredible ways, so much so that they profoundly changed and developed you as a person. You are different now in terms of how you were before you knew them. They took you into realms of experiencing the world that you didn't know before.

Write their names on the white sections in the picture. In talking about aspects of your life story, these people must feature, and be celebrated and applauded.

■Development

The participant may like to write little thank-you notes to their 'Knights' or bring photos of these people to make a collage of them to put up on their wall. This will serve as a reminder of how what these people did for them lives on inside them every day, as vital internal resources that help them live their life well and to the full.

Figure 3.5

Further reading

Holt-Lunstad, J., Smith, T. B., Baker, M., Harris, T. and Stephenson, D. (2015) Loneliness and social isolation as risk factors for mortality: A meta-analytic review.*Perspect. Psychol. Sci.*, March, 10(2): 227–237.

Johnson, K. V. A. and Dunbar, R. I. M. (2016) Pain tolerance predicts human social network size. *Scientific Reports* 6: 25267.

Panksepp, J. and Biven, L. (2012) *The Archaeology of Mind: Neuroevolutionary origins of human emotion.* New York: W. W. Norton & Co.

Sunderland, M. (2016) *What Every Parent Needs to Know.* London: Dorling Kindersley.

Teo, A. (2015) Does mode of contact with different types of social relationships predict depression among older adults? Evidence from a nationally representative survey. *Journal of the American Geriatrics Society*, October.

Ybarra, O., Burnstein, E., Winkielman, P., Keller, M. C., Manis, M., Chan, E. and Rodriguez, J. (2008) Mental exercising through simple socializing: Social interaction promotes general cognitive functioning. *Pers. Soc. Psychol. Bull.*, February, 34(2): 248–259.

Love hurts

■Essential theory

We inherit grief just by virtue of being born human.

(Euripides, 431 BC)

The loss of a relationship, experiences of rejection and feelings of not belonging can cause intense emotional pain. Whether we like it or not, we are all genetically programmed to need close emotional bonds. Bonding behaviour, known as attachment, is not simply something that occurs only in childhood. It continues throughout life. Our attachment style is formed on the basis of whether we loved in peace in childhood due to consistent warm empathic responsiveness from parents and carers (known as secure attachment) or whether we loved in torment (due to on–off responses and/or too many mis-attuned, un-empathic, frightening or cruel responses).

Attachment is a vital psycho-biochemical reality (Panksepp and Biven, 2012). It determines so much of our social and emotional development, our self-worth and our very perception of life. Insecure attachment often leaves us feeling that life is a threatening journey. Secure attachment means it often feels like the most amazing and privileged adventure. If we have had painful childhood experiences and so deny or try to defend against our need to bond, sooner or later we will move into a sense of something major missing in our life and feelings of hopelessness and/or depression. Isolation is as bad for physical health as smoking 15 cigarettes a day (Holt-Lunstad et al., 2015).

Yet some people are unaware of our genetically programmed need for attachment. They may perhaps make strong attachments to objects rather than to people, e.g. their car, their house, their computer. They may throw themselves into work, pursuing success and money. At some stage in their life, however, they will realise that these are false quests and empty alternatives which cannot protect them from a deep sense of meaninglessness. As Freud said: 'Those who cannot love, fall ill'. It's vital that professionals understand this huge hormonal force called attachment, why some people try to deny it, and what happens if they do.

The attachment system is deep in the mammalian part of our brain. It is known by neuroscientists as the CARE system (Panksepp and Biven, 2012). The key emotion chemicals of this system are opioids, oxytocin and prolactin. When a loving relationship has strongly activated these chemicals in our brain, we feel a deep sense of peace and calm. We feel safe enough in the world to want to be creative, to explore, learn, play and relate to others. But when we lose the person who makes us feel like this or lose their love (or fear that we have), the pain is awful. This is caused by an 'opioid withdrawal' and an activation of various pain centres in the brain. All too often this means a rollercoaster of intense feelings of rage, betrayal, grief and depression. Opioid withdrawal can also make animals behave very nastily to each other and/or fall into a terrible depression. Because of this biochemically evidenced pain, some people, after experiencing loss, try to cut off from their attachment needs and put a wall around their hearts. As a result, they dare not love any more in any long-term committed way, and yet the price of this is usually a feeling of emptiness, hopelessness and/or a flat depression. To avoid this, many people try to compensate by having an often-insatiable desire for material possessions, the latest clothes, gadgets, or develop some form of addiction to screen time, etc. Here are some more scientific examples of why the pain of loss hurts so much.

■The brain's distress system (the PANIC/GRIEF system)

When we feel rejected, lose someone or their love, or fear we have, then the PANIC/GRIEF system in the lower mammalian brain is activated. Scientists can artificially stimulate with electrodes this system in young mammals, causing them to howl for their mothers (Panksepp and Biven, 2012). The panic aspect of this system is particularly in evidence in children, who scream and scream if they can't find their mummy or they have to let her go.

The activation of the PANIC/GRIEF system means opioid withdrawal in a key part of the brain known as the anterior cingulate.

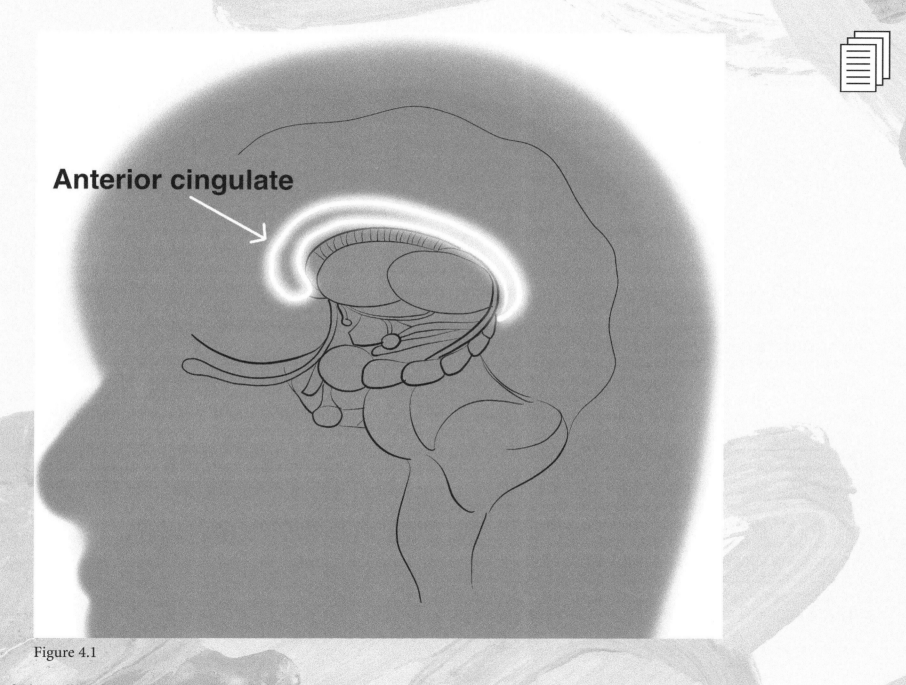

Figure 4.1

When opioids are optimally activated in the brain they can naturally diminish fear and anxiety. So with opioid withdrawal from feelings of loss, rejection, not belonging, fear and anxiety can all too easily flood the bodymind. A world-leading researcher in neuroscience, Professor Jaak Panksepp (1998), compared coming off heroin (which taps into the brain's opioid system) to relationship break-up. Because both activate the same painful processes in the brain, they are remarkably similar in effect. Each usually leaves the person with extreme emotional pain, depression, over- or under-eating, sleep problems, crying or wishing to cry, irritability or aggressiveness.

■ Love made angry

All too frequently in the news we hear about 'love made angry'. When we look at the brain chemistry of broken hearts, this is not at all surprising.

Pain in love results in the following:

- *Increased activation of acetylcholine.* When there is a withdrawal of opioids in the brain, then what is known as 'opponent forces' are released. These opponent forces involve the release of high levels of a chemical called acetylcholine. At optimal levels, acetylcholine can help us concentrate and feel alert. But at high levels acetylcholine can make people angry, hostile and attacking.
- *Increased activation of the brain chemical corticotrophin releasing factor (CRF).* This in turn activates high levels of stress hormones (one of which is cortisol) into the brain and body. These can block the release of positive arousal chemicals (including dopamine, opioids, oxytocin). It also activates stress response systems in the brain, leading to depression, anxiety disorders and/or problems with aggression.
- *Increased activation of glutamate.* Strong activation of glutamate can dramatically increase crying. If high levels of glutamate are artificially activated in the brain, the comforting effects of such things as music and lovely company are lost.
- *Decreased levels of serotonin.* Low serotonin can increase aggressive impulses, hence some of the angry outbursts of people with broken hearts, jealous feelings or threat of loss. Also, due to the depletion of serotonin, (mood stabiliser), people are wide open to impulsive outbursts of irritation, anger, rage or attacks on the self (as in self-harm).

Not all of us move from loss to aggression, but if you have a poor ability to reflect, think and calm down after stress, you are particularly vulnerable (Chester et al., 2013).

What to do when the brain is set on love made angry

The physical comforting of grief will release opioids and oxytocin in the brain. These will then bring acetylcholine levels back down to base rate. This is why it is vital for children and adults alike who are suffering from the pain of loss, rejection and not belonging (even if on the surface they look just fine) to receive comfort. Schools in particular need to be aware of children who have lost a parent or who are 'loving in torment' at home. So many children suffering the pain of loss or rejection behave in very angry or aggressive ways because of their changed brain chemistry. Tragically, it's then all too easy for people to start to hate them, punish them and want to exclude them rather than help them. Hopefully, increasing public knowledge about these dramatic changes in brain chemistry will help to improve levels of compassion in society so children are helped at school instead of being permanently excluded because they are grieving.

■ Many angry people need help to feel sad

One of the most important life skills is knowing how to suffer well and grieve well. If we don't have this skill, then the cost to self and others can be very high indeed. Research shows that sometimes people and animals do actually die of a broken heart (Goodall, 1990; Martikainen and Valkonen, 1996). Parents who have not been helped to work through the painful losses and separations that they have experienced in their lives may find that their parenting is adversely affected as a result of their grief. Their children may start to develop emotional or behavioural problems. When they go into counselling or therapy, their child's problems often completely stop.

■The use of the exercises in the book to help a person grieve well

The exercises are designed to support children, teenagers and adults in a healthy grief process. Some offer vital psycho-education as above whereas others provide ways of heightening awareness as the first step to grieving well.

Museum of hurt

■Objective

Having been deeply hurt, it is all too easy for people to harden their hearts and/or cut off from their distress and pain. But the costs can be great:

- Cutting off from your own pain often means cutting off from that of others and hence may block your compassion and concern.
- Research shows that those who bottle up their feelings are at least a third more likely to die young compared with people who express what they feel. Risks increased by 47 per cent for heart disease and 70 per cent for cancer (Chapman et al., 2013).
- As Freud said, feelings pushed down into the unconscious 'simply proliferate in the dark' (1915). The result can be very debilitating neurotic symptoms.

This exercise is therefore designed to support the participant in staying open to the pain, so that they can start to work it through. It is hoped that the containing function of the images will help the participant to feel safe enough to do so.

■Instructions to give the participant

The importance of grieving loss is recognised. Yet the major hurts in one's life also need working through. When someone has been really hurt, they can move into feeling their pain or cutting off from it. The latter can come with a major price tag that often entails physical or neurotic symptoms and becoming less compassionate towards the pain and distress of others. Look at each exhibit in turn. Think of times or events in your life when you have felt very hurt. Choose an exhibit stand in this museum of hurt that is appropriate to your various hurtful experiences. For example, choose the 'ouch' stand for a little hurt and one of the others for a major

hurt. Think of a title or phrase to describe the event and write this by the exhibit. What was the worst thing about it? What do you want the person who hurt you to know or understand? Try saying it to them now as if they were in the room.

- 'What I want you to know is . . . '
- 'I am so hurt that you . . . '
- 'I feel so angry because you . . . '

■Development

Ask the participant to focus on particular hurts in the museum, those that are the most emotionally charged. Ask them to use clay to make a sculpture of the hurt or ask them to do a sandplay about it. It may help to use these different modes of expression as each offers a different perspective and different form of working through.

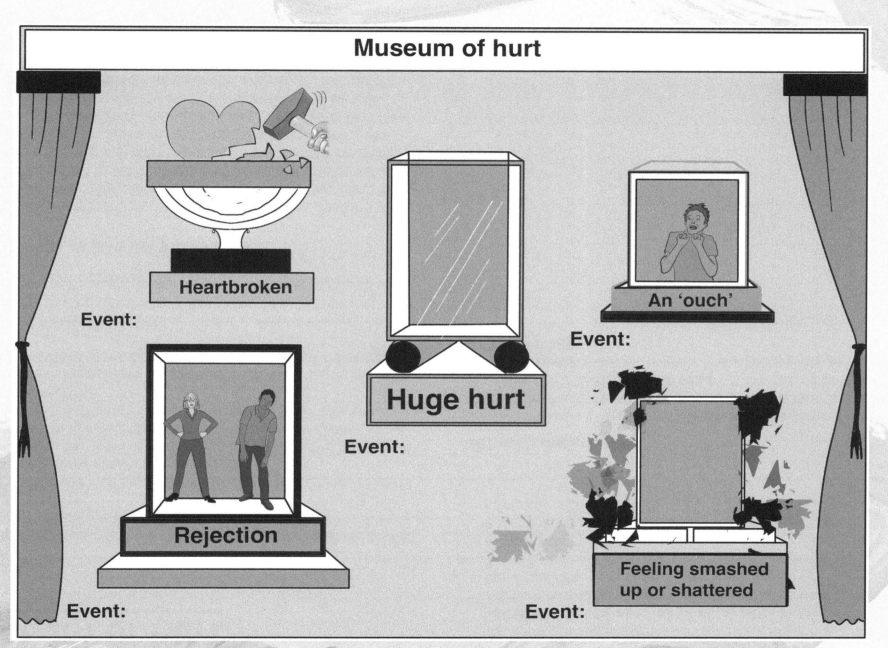

Figure 4.2

When I can't reach you

■Objective

It can be intensely lonely to be in a relationship with someone who is not willing to say what they feel, to be vulnerable, open and undefended, especially when you are willing to be. That said, sometimes people are unreachable because they experience the person who is trying to reach them as too pushy, intrusive, needy or demanding in some way.

This exercise is designed for the participant who has an important relationship with someone whom they often experience as unreachable in some important way. The hope is that the exercise will bring about a heightened awareness of the situation, as the first stage to considered action. The exercise can also provide a vehicle for the participant to speak about his or her pain, hurt and aloneness when trying to reach someone who seems so unreachable.

■Instructions to give the participant

Do you have an important relationship with someone who seems or is unreachable in some way? It could be someone who keeps making excuses about not being able to meet up. Or it may be someone who is physically present but emotionally absent, someone who does not tell you what they are feeling, or who finds it very difficult to express the more vulnerable human feelings such as hurt, need, yearning, love, disappointment and fear.

On the picture choose the wall or door that speaks most accurately about how you feel when this person shuts you out or becomes unreachable (physically and/or emotionally). Change the images in any way you like to make them more accurate: for example, make the wall thicker or enlarge the 'Keep Out' sign.

Draw yourself in the picture if you like in terms of where you are in relation to the barriers between you. Now write on the 'message sending' paper aeroplane or the little letter in the picture the things you want the unreachable person to know.

Ask yourself why you think the person is unreachable. Do they avoid intimacy? Or are they in a flight/withdrawal defence mode because you are being somewhat needy, demanding or intrusive? Has someone in their past hurt them and so led to their mistrust in some way? How might you need to be with this person so that they feel safer to be 'reached' by you? What other clarifications or insights about your relationship have you gained by doing this task?

■Development – Grieving over what could have been but wasn't

People who have or have had an important relationship with someone who is cut off from their emotions or is unreachable often need time to grieve over the lost potential of a relationship that at some point promised so much but in actuality could not grow and develop. It will be useful to introduce the concept of 'lost hope'.

When I can't reach you

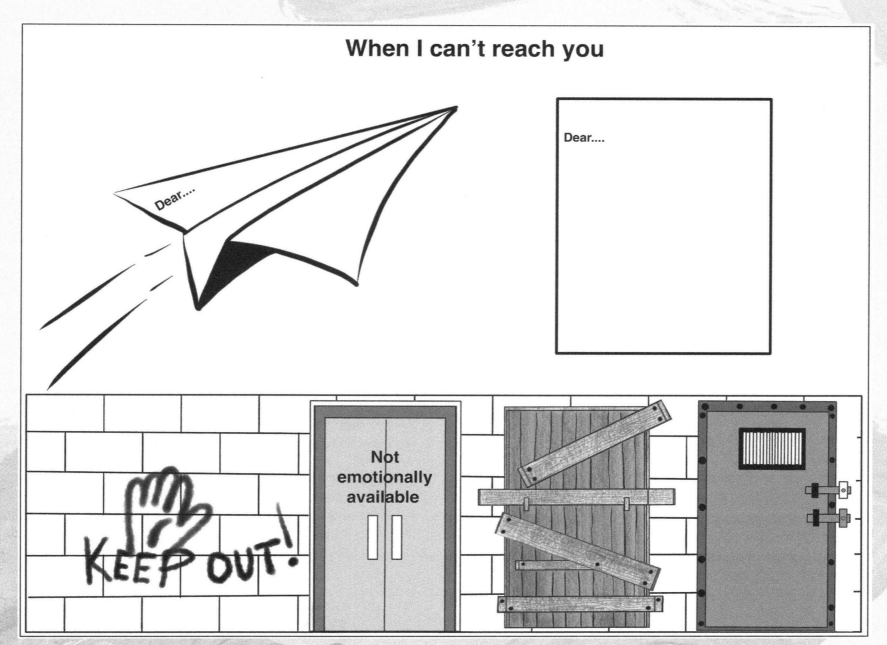

Figure 4.3

Life after losing a person or their love

■Objective

When you lose a person you love or you lose their love, someone who has been a key part of your world (especially your mate or your child), the perception of many other things in your life can be dramatically affected. You can begin to look at life through spectacles coloured by desolation, hurt, pain and anger. It is vital that people work through their pain and loss in order not to suffer from depression, anxiety or ongoing bitterness.

When children who have suffered a loss do not grieve in the presence of a comforting other, they often move from pain to anger or violence. This is because uncomforted grief changes brain chemistry, activating high levels of acetylcholine. Particularly in those people who aren't able to emotionally regulate well, this chemical imbalance can trigger feelings of anger and hostility. Also, without help, grief that is denied, un-mourned or unworked through can result in all manner of physical symptoms. In fact, hopelessness and depression are a key risk for heart disease and death (Anda et al., 1993). Moreover, we all need help to work through feelings after significant loss. There are no exceptions. Sadly, people who feel they can manage without help all too often turn to alternative 'help' and self-medication, e.g. alcohol, over-eating, drugs, self-harm. This exercise provides some language for grief, describing common and natural feelings resulting from loss. Finding the right words can be a vital first step for people to begin their mourning process.

■Instructions to give the participant

After a painful loss it is vital that people feel their grief and talk to others who understand what they are going through, rather than cutting off or bottling up their feelings. Research shows that un-mourned grief can badly affect physical and mental health, one's parenting capacity and the ability to live life well. In this sense, people can get stuck in grief. In contrast, speaking about loss in the presence of a warm, empathic other heals.

Look at the picture. Tick any of the images that convey what life feels like without this person, or without their love. If none of the images are right for you, draw your own in the empty boxes provided. Which of the images speak most clearly about your pain?

■Development

The best development would be to continue, if appropriate, with the next exercise in the book – 'The end of the relationship: What now?'

Life after losing a person or their love

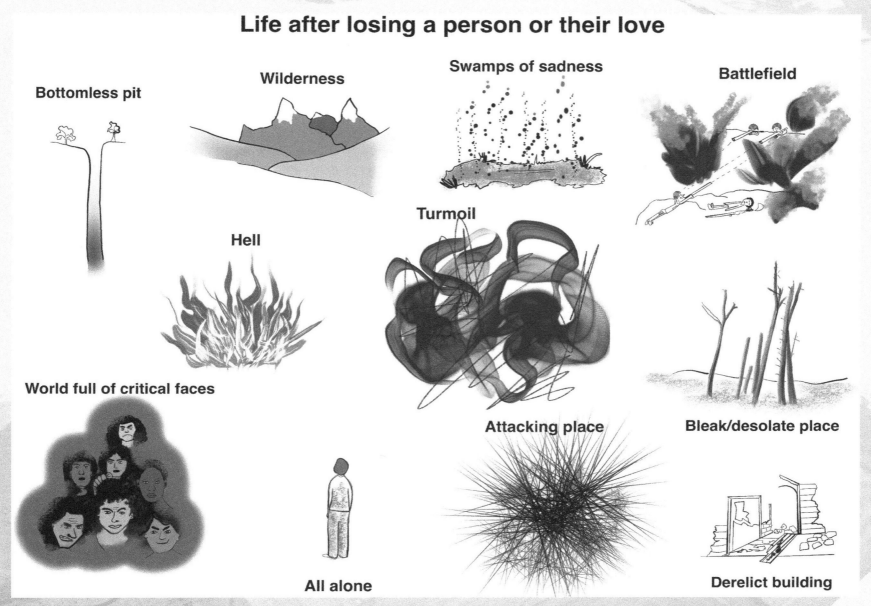

Figure 4.4

The end of a relationship: What now?

■ Objective

When a key relationship in your life ends, it can feel like a part of you has died, your life has ended and/or everything seems pointless now. Due to the sheer pain of the feelings of loss it can be difficult to think well, because feelings are flooding the thinking part of the brain. So this exercise is to support the participant to let both their irrational voice and rational voice have a say. When worst fantasies are written down (rather than left swirling around and around in one's mind as awful ruminations), it can be a good way to address them and check them against reality, particularly if you are doing this in the presence of a thinking, compassionate other.

■ Instructions to give the participant

Now that this important relationship in your life has ended and it's so painful, it's really good to stand back and ask, 'What next?' On the picture, write down your worst fantasies about what might happen next in your life. Then on the 'Coping strategies' circle write down what you will never lose, what can never be taken away, namely your resources, your strengths, good ideas for where to go for comfort, who to spend time with and the lovely memories about the relationship which should not be tarred just because the relationship has ended, etc.

When you have done this, stand back. Imagine the 'worst fantasies' were written by a child version of you. Talk to her. What would you say to reassure her? How are happenings in your childhood colouring and increasing the pain you are feeling now?

■ Development – Loss

Offer the following quotations to the participant. Explain that most of the statements were written by famous authors or poets, all of whom had suffered the loss of a loved one. Discuss which quotations the participant can relate to and why.

1 'Her absence is like the sky, spread over everything.' (C. S. Lewis, 1966)
2 'Comforter, where, where is your comforting?' (Gerard Manley Hopkins, in Gardner, 1970)
3 'Water, water everywhere nor any drop to drink.' (S. T. Coleridge, 1992)
4 'The degree to which he had suppressed violent feelings . . . only hit him when he opened the linen basket in the bathroom, a week later, and found a brassiere, a pair of pants, a petticoat, coiled at the bottom like snakes ready to strike. That was the first time, taken by surprise, that he had tears in his eyes. Howl then, he told himself, standing in the bathroom with ghosts of her habitation in his square fingers, go on, howl. He could not.' (Daniel after the sudden death of his wife in A. S. Byatt's *Still Life*, 1997)
5 'I'd walk down and I'd stare at the house for ages . . . I'd keep saying it in my head – "He's dead, he's dead, he's dead". But it didn't mean anything.' (Rosemary Dinnage, 1990)
6 'What helps in breaking up is a reminder that there isn't much to do except to grieve and hurt.' (Susie Orbach, 1994)

Figure 4.5

Loving someone who isn't good at loving

Then come to me. I will give you a cold, cold kiss.
My roses are dead. My lips are grey. My eyes
Have neither iris nor pupil. They died, and now all is white;
White in a face of stone. Sister, cold lover, come.

(John Alexander Chapman, b. 1875,
Gipsy Queen, in Ricks, 1999)

■Objective

Many people who love someone who isn't good at loving fall into the same trap. They try so hard to awaken the love in the other by all manner of self-sacrifice, overgenerous acts, compliance and over-tolerance. Sadly, this process often results in them putting their own development on hold. In relentless attempts to awaken love in the other person, they can unwittingly enter into a life of emotional deprivation. Furthermore, in a desperate attempt to please, they may stifle those aspects of themselves which the other person criticises and attacks, e.g. their passion, drives, dreams, ambitions. Another common pitfall is to be over-cheerful, in an attempt to compensate for the life and joy that may be lacking in the other person, or in the relationship generally. Yet all this tends to bring just more and more defeat and disappointment. They keep coming up against the restrictions that the other person places on love and intimacy, which prevent the relationship from becoming in any way emotionally nourishing.

■Instructions to give the participant

Think of a person who really matters to you and who is a key part of your life. On the table laid out with a feast, colour in all the things that you want from this person who really matters to you. Now turn to the tables next to it. On the 'What am I actually getting?' table or the 'Relationship as famine' table (if it feels right to use this table) draw or write what this person is actually 'laying on your table', so to speak.

Are you loving someone who isn't good at relationships or isn't good at loving? Or are you loving someone who doesn't really love you? Armstrong-Perlman speaks eloquently of the allure and the pain of loving someone who isn't good at loving. Does this describe your situation in any way?

When they speak about their relationship, one wonders at their blindness. There had been indications that the other was incapable of reciprocating or loving or accepting them in the way they desire. They had been pursuing an alluring but rejecting other, an exciting yet frustrating other. The [person] initially may have offered conditions of hope but it fails to satisfy. It has awakened an intensity of yearning, but is essentially the elusive object of desire, seemingly there but just out of reach.

(Armstrong-Perlman, 1991)

■Development

For some participants, in order to prevent them taking so personally the deficit they are receiving from the other person, and blaming themselves ('I guess I am just not loveable'), it may be useful to reflect on possible causes. You may discuss together how some people who have been very hurt can cut off from the loving part of themselves. Hurtful childhoods often include all manner of betrayals, agonising hurt, loss, lack of empathy and compassion, leaving a person not daring to really love again (in a deep, committed way). With others, the loving part of themselves simply didn't develop in the first place, as they were not truly loved as a child. The participant could then think about the past of the person they feel so hurt by, so that they can differentiate between their own lovableness and the other person's incapacity to love.

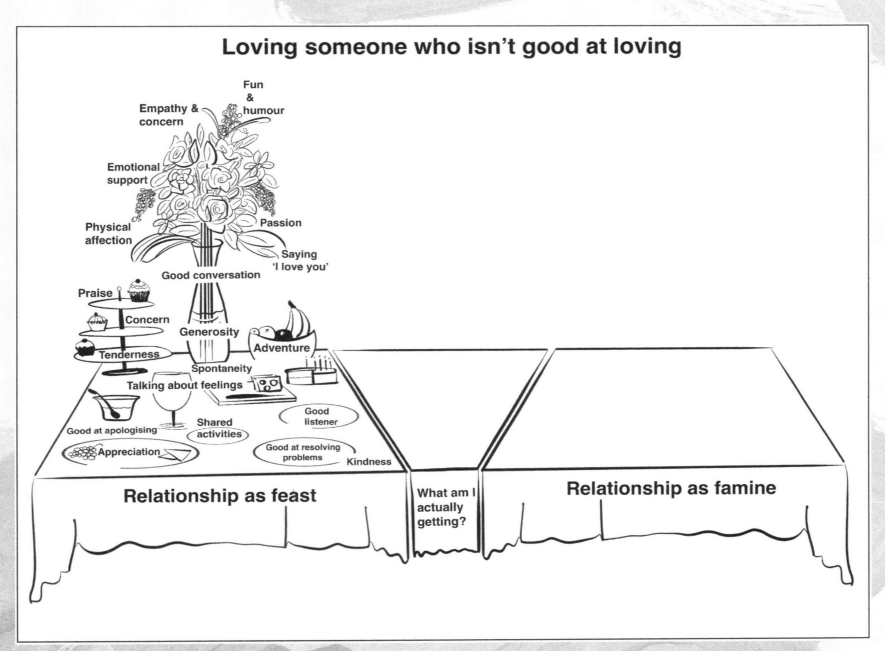

Loving someone who isn't good at loving

Fun & humour

Empathy & concern

Emotional support

Physical affection

Passion

Saying 'I love you'

Good conversation

Praise

Concern

Generosity

Tenderness

Adventure

Spontaneity

Talking about feelings

Good at apologising

Shared activities

Good listener

Appreciation

Good at resolving problems

Kindness

Relationship as feast

What am I actually getting?

Relationship as famine

Figure 4.6

Do I matter to you?

■Objective

It's key to the human condition that we need to know that we really matter to the people who matter to us. And yet, people are sometimes accused of being unreasonable and needy when they get angry about not getting enough time and attention from their loved ones. However, a famous relationship researcher and couple therapist calls this anger a perfectly natural 'attachment protest' (Johnson, 2017). Attachment protest is not pathological. In fact, as Sue Johnson explains, all angry reposts such as, 'You are so selfish' or 'You never think about my needs' are fuelled by this core underlying human need to know that we matter to the people who matter to us. Where it goes wrong is when this need is so thwarted or threatened that people move into panic and fear and then lash out in verbal rage. This drives the other person further away from them rather than drawing them closer.

Meanwhile, being honest about our vulnerability often has the opposite effect. For example, we could just say, 'I am frightened that I don't matter to you because you didn't say a proper hello when you came in from work and instead you went straight to your emails'. Most people with a heart and who do care would listen and respond well to such a brave disclosure.

Children often express their attachment protests through challenging behaviours rather than through angry accusation. When their recognition needs (Berne, 1979) are not being met, they often then do something provocative just to ensure the adult/carer/teacher relates to them, engages with them and acknowledges them. It is well documented that children feel that negative attention to satisfy recognition needs is always better than no attention at all.

The exercise aims to heighten awareness of the participant's attachment protests and to normalise these. This is with the hope that the participant will then be able to find ways of expressing their protests in close relationships in healthier ways, which do not blast the other person away from them but instead lead to fruitful and honest conversation.

■Instructions to give the participant

An integral part of feeling secure in close relationships is to know that we really matter to the other person. When we feel insecure about this, we can move into what is known as an 'attachment protest' (Johnson, 2017). This is a perfectly normal and healthy expression. However, for the protest to be heard it needs to be expressed in ways that do not make the other person feel criticised.

Think of times when you have screamed, shouted or spoken in a hateful tone of voice your attachment protest through blaming or accusation, e.g. 'You are never there for me' or 'You prefer your computer to me, you selfish so and so'. Write all your primitive, angry statements and protest screams in the 'Do I matter to you? Blame Box'.

Then in the memory theatres draw or write any childhood memories you have of not feeling sure how much you mattered to a parent, or of feeling particularly wobbly as to whether you were loved or not. Consider how these painful memories may be fuelling your panic and fear in the present, which are driving you to express your attachment protest with blame and attack.

Now think of how you can make attachment protests in your relationships now and/or in the future in a way that does not blast the other person away from you but draws them closer to you. In the 'Wanting to resolve box' write what you could say to a key person in your life to check out how much you matter, but leave out all the blame and attack. For example:

- 'When you say you were too tired to go out for a meal with me the other night I had a fear that I don't really matter to you. Can I check that out?'
- 'At least once a week will you tell me more clearly how important I am to you?'
- 'Will you let me know that I matter to you by doing?'

■Development

One key development exercise would be to ask the participant to complete the next exercise – 'No one listens/too unhelped'.

Blame box

Do I matter to you?

Do I matter to you?
From yearning to screaming

Wanting to resolve box

Do I matter to you?

Memory theatre

Memory theatre

Memory theatre

Figure 4.7

No one listens / too unhelped

■Objective

Most people remember times in their life when they felt utterly alone because no one listened, understood, showed any interest in how they were feeling, or helped when in fact they could have helped. Such painful events leave a lasting impression whether in such contexts as a breach of trust, a betrayal, a time of catastrophic aloneness, an awful disappointment or let-down, a painful put-down, or a realisation that the other person is incapable of understanding something you desperately needed them to understand.

At times, these failed connections can be negative turning points in an ongoing relationship with a family member, friend or partner. These 'attachment ruptures', as named by famous couple therapist Sue Johnson (2004), happen in a time of real need, when the other person's emotional blindness can sometimes by experienced as breaking the relationship in some way. Furthermore, from such painful failed connections, a person may form negative core beliefs about themselves and others such as 'I'm not worth listening to', 'I can never get people to understand me', or 'My needs are unimportant'. These can inform the way they live their lives.

This exercise is therefore designed to focus on unforgettable moments of failed connection, so that they can be reflected on, grieved, acknowledged as deeply significant in the course of a life by the listening other, and worked through. Then, if appropriate and possible, they can be resolved with the other person.

■Instructions to give the participant

Times of profound connection, misconnection and failed connection with people who were or are important in our lives form vital aspects of our life story. We never forget them. Things change during those times for better or for worse. It is important that these times are not just pushed away into our memory store but rather shared with a listening other so that they can be fully made sense of and worked through.

Think of a memory or memories of painful times in your life when you felt utterly alone because of a failed connection with another person. They did not try to understand what you were feeling, they did not ask you what you were feeling, and they could have helped but didn't.

Now look at the picture. In the Memories circle, write a title for each of the memories you have chosen as if they were book titles. Then write in the box provided what you would have liked to have happened at the time but which didn't.

■Discussion topic – Connections and misconnections in the arts

Participants can now talk about moments of connection as these need to be heard just as much as those misconnections. To enrich the dialogue, you might like to ask the participant to think of books, plays or films they know where there have been memorable moments of connection or misconnection (e.g. *Lost in Translation*, *Remains of the Day*, *Othello*, *Romeo and Juliet*) and how these have resonated with their own experiences.

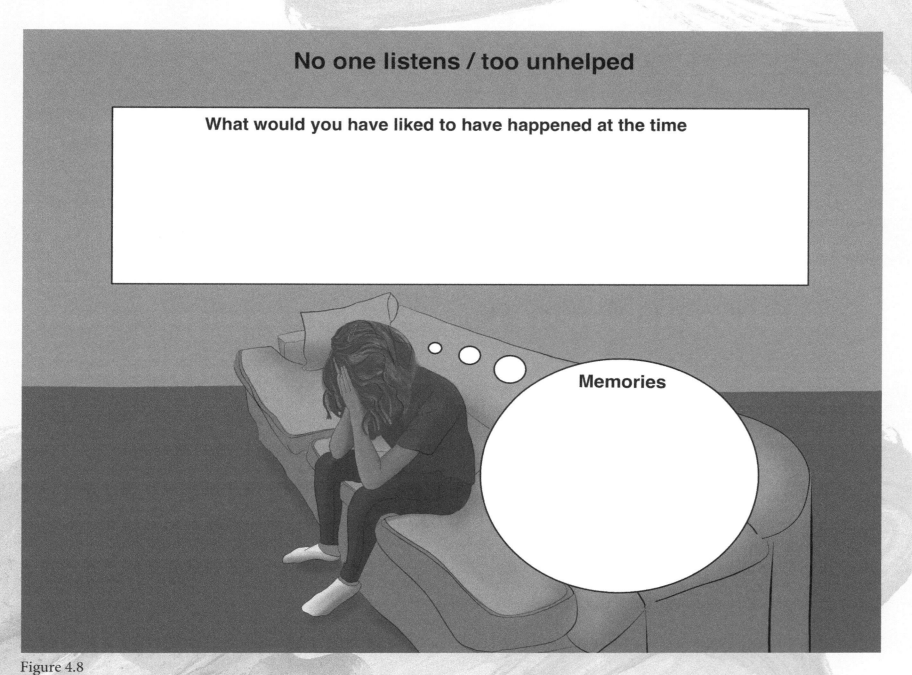

Figure 4.8

Rejected / not wanted / uninvited / redundant

Experiences of social rejection can trigger some of the worst pain we know. In fact, sometimes just one incident of rejection in childhood can lead to long-term social phobias: fear of meeting new people, or going to parties, etc. Why is it that these negative social experiences have such an awful effect on us? Research shows that feelings of rejection and underlying sense of social disconnection trigger the same centres in the brain as those which trigger when we are in physical pain (Eisenberger, 2012).

Many people who suffered such experiences in childhood are still feeling the negative effects years later. This is because they have never been properly talked about and worked through with a listening other who can correct any negative self-beliefs. So this exercise gives a forum for that.

■Instructions to give the participant

Ask the participant to scan their life history for moments when they felt rejected, not wanted or uninvited. On the white slats on the door in the picture, ask the participant to write the first memories that came into their head. Ask them what they felt about themselves at the time. Did they manage to keep their self-esteem intact and realise that the rejection was far more about the other person's failings than their own, e.g. intolerance of difference? If their self-esteem remains blighted by the incidents, which they still are taking very personally, ask the participant if they would be prepared to speak now to the rejecters as if they were in the room, with the 'finish the sentence' technique. If so, ask them to finish the sentences:

What I feel about you is . . .
I feel angry because . . .

I feel sad because . . .
I took what you did personally because . . .

As practitioner, you may need to correct them if they are still moving into self-blame for the incidents and support them to find appropriate empowered anger instead.

■Development

Some participants may not know that, all too often, outside of conscious awareness, we pick friends or partners who treat us in emotionally neglectful or abusive ways; similar to those we have known in our past. If this is relevant to participants and they find this interesting, perhaps refer to Freud's concept of 'repetition compulsion', which means a pull to repeat the past, even when it's bad. We still don't quite know why this happens, but the belief is that the mind is trying to work things through, and so processes the pain by repeating. You might give examples to the participant of people who have experienced repetition compulsion caused by rejection and social disconnection. Here are two actual examples you could use. A woman, whose mother had her by accident and never really wanted children, found that she always picked partners who left her because 'she wasn't interesting enough'. A man had an alcoholic father. He always felt he was far less interesting to his father than the father's bottles of drink. In adulthood the man found a lovely partner only to discover after a while that this partner too had an addiction, not to drink but to gambling. This left the man feeling just as he did with his alcoholic father – not of central importance.

Rejected / not wanted / uninvited / redundant

Figure 4.9

On the outside of the group

■Objective

Being in groups is often such an emotive subject, and too many of us never get someone to listen to us about our experiences of groups across a lifetime. This is the main objective of this exercise. How we are in groups often resembles how we were in our original family group. If you have had painful experiences in the family group, the pain is often re- triggered in group experiences later on in life, particularly when you feel not accepted by a group, not wanted or on the outside looking in. So the objective of this exercise is to work through painful experiences of groups but also holding in mind the original group – one's family.

■Instructions to give the participant

Ask the participant to think of times when they felt outside of a group now or in the past. People might think of experiences of being bullied at school, feeling outside of groups of parents chatting together when collecting their children from school, not being accepted by their family. Ask them what they felt/feel at the time and what they have 'learnt' about themselves or others as a result. If what they have 'learnt' is self-denigrating you will need to draw their attention to this and voice other realities, e.g. that the group was insensitive or outright rejecting rather than the situation being about their failings.

If the participant has clear interest in this exercise, you could then ask them if they would be willing to consider this group experience in terms of how it might be a repeat in some way of their original group, namely their family. In other words, they may be interested to compare their feelings and coping mechanisms with these painful group experiences to those in their original family. If by doing the exercise, participants find that they seem to be playing limiting or unhealthy roles in groups (e.g. they are often on the outside of a group or the one who can't get their voice heard), they could be encouraged to discuss ways of changing how they are in groups in the future in order to get a different response and a better experience.

■Development

Many participants will appreciate you listening to them about how they were in their first group (their family), particularly if it resembles how they are in groups now. Some participants may also appreciate talking more generally about groups and their effect, by thinking of films, books, plays, actual historical events, particularly those which have some resonance with their own experience of groups. I have found some participants to draw useful analogies for their own experiences of groups with those depicted in William Golding's *Lord of the Flies*; the effect of the Nazi party on the young people of Germany; the feelings involved in actively supporting a particular football team or religious group; and occasions of mass hysteria in crowds.

You might also like to discuss common themes in groups: how, for example, many groups need to have a scapegoat or an opposing group as an enemy or target to give them a purpose and make them feel more united. Talk about group norms, taboos and sanctions. Look at stages in the life of a group, e.g. forming, norming, storming, performing and mourning.

On the outside of the group

Figure 4.10

Further reading

Anda, R., Williamson, D., Jones, D., Macera, C., Eaker, E., Glassman, A. and Marks, J. (1993) Depressed affect, hopelessness, and the risk of ischemic heart disease in a cohort of U.S. adults. Epidemiology,July, 4(4): 285–294.

Chapman, B. P., Fiscella, K., Kawachi, I., Duberstein, P. and Muennig, P. (2013) Emotion suppression and mortality risk over a 12-year follow-up. *J. Psychosom. Res.*, October, 75(4): 381–385.

Chester, D., Eisenberger, N., Pond, R., Richman, S., Bushman, B. and DeWall, C. (2013) The interactive effect of social pain and executive functioning on aggression: An fMRI experiment. *Social Cognitive and Affective Neuroscience*, 1–6. Available at: www.ncbi.nlm.nih.gov/pmc/articles/ PMC4014110/.

Eisenberger, N. (2012) The pain of social disconnection: examining the shared neural underpinnings of physical and social pain. *Nat. Rev. Neurosci.*, May, 13(6): 421–434.

Holt-Lunstad, J., Smith, T., Baker, M., Harris, T. and Stephenson, D. (2015) Loneliness and social isolation as risk factors for mortality: A meta-analytic review.*Perspect. Psychol. Sci.*, March, 10(2): 227–237.

Johnson, S. (2017) *Becoming an Emotionally Focused Couple Therapist: The workbook*, London: Routledge.

Damaging and destructive relationships

■About this chapter

When relationships go well they can transport us to the heights of exhilaration or deep states of calm and feelings of well-being. When they go badly, they can do the opposite, causing us the most unbearable pain and not only compromising mental health but also physical health. So the exercises in this chapter are designed to help the participant become more aware, as the first step to change, of those destructive relationships and damaging patterns of relating that they have in their life (past or present). Many of the exercises provide vital psycho-education to support the participant to make informed decisions about any changes they want to make in their relationships.

■Essential theory

Some relationships become breeding grounds for destructive behaviour, bringing both parties misery and suffering. In many cases, the negative modes of interaction were learnt in their own childhoods where there was no modelling of healthy conflict resolution, only negative patterns of blame and criticism. In other cases, the interactions are fuelled by the discharging of years of rage and hate towards people in the past, particularly in respect of relationships they had with their parents and other key adults when they were children.

Some destructive energies come in the form of repeated commands, criticism, put-downs, humiliations and shaming. In fact, famous couple therapist and researcher John Gottman found that he could predict with great accuracy those couples who would divorce shortly after marrying. The four lethal modes of relating were: 1) defensiveness; 2) stone-walling; 3) criticism; and 4) contempt. Interestingly he found that, in their silent treatment of their partner, the stone-wallers (85 per cent of them were men) may look cool and collected on the outside but actually had a very rapid heartbeat (of over 100 beats per minute) during the stone-walling (Gottman, 2012). Research shows that repeated destructive arguments with a partner (using these four modes of relating) are not only bad for your emotional health but also for your physical health; they can adversely affect your immune system and interfere with body mechanisms that prevent us from getting cancer (Jaremka et al., 2013).

Destructive relationships are often also marked by a death of the finer human relational capacities such as tenderness, compassion, soothing, expressing appreciation, compliments, quality listening time, real curiosity in the other, laughing together, fun and play. In such relationships, destructive energies are also likely to keep the emotional development of both parties at a standstill.

■Different forms of destructive behaviour in close relationships

Human beings are creative in the sheer range of ways in which they can cause hurt to another in their relationships. Here are just a few examples.

Nagging

Persistent nagging can make people contract into a defensive and self-protective way of being in the world. No amount of moaning, blaming or criticising has ever won over another person. In fact, it often does just the opposite. Over time, persistent nagging can mean a build-up of resentment and hate in the nagged at person, which can then be 'cashed in' in some way, such as ending the relationship or having an affair. This is not surprising, as being nagged means persistently being told how you are failing.

Naggers are often unaware that they are often applying the critical voices in their own heads to other people. Many have ruthlessly high standards, which no one could ever live up to. Children's lives can be made a misery and the atmosphere in the home spoilt by telling them how flawed and failing they are.

The unconscious message is: 'Be more perfect – because I am failing to live up to my own inner critical voices, which demand perfection from me'.

Radiating gloom

Radiating gloom (Horney, 1992) is all about putting more and more negative energy into the atmosphere. It can be carried out through cold silences, bad moods and acting out your resentment through things like heavy sighs, weary facial expressions or even acts such as loud, intrusive vacuuming. It can also be done through persistent moaning about life, the future, the state of the country, the traffic, etc. Radiating gloom can blight the creative energy and optimism of even the most resilient of people. Underlying punitive elements often involve some form of 'If I feel awful, why shouldn't you?'

Guilt tripping

Guilt tripping is persecuting the other person from a victim position of 'poor me'. In other words, one person persecutes by making the other feel awful about themselves in the face of the aggressor's martyrdom or woundedness. This form of attack is often chosen as a form of expressing angry feelings used by the aggressor's own parent. Here are some examples:

- 'If it weren't for you . . .'
- 'After all I have done for you and all the sacrifices I have made for you, you go and treat me like that.'
- [Looking pained and exhausted] 'You go out. I'll stay at home and babysit again. But don't bother about me, dear, you just enjoy yourself.'
- 'How could you be late again, when you know how much I needed you to be on time?'
- 'You've ruined everything now!'
- 'You've ruined my life.'

Passive aggression

Passive aggression is a way of indirectly expressing hostility through passivity, inaction, and frustrating the recipient. For example, when the other person says,

'Can we sort this out?', the passive-aggressive person may reply with something like 'I don't know what there is to talk about'. Other passive-aggressive behaviours include the following:

- Saying 'Pardon?' when you've heard perfectly well
- 'Forgetting' such things as anniversaries, birthdays or errands, which you know really matter to the other person
- Being late (particularly when you know she or he can't stand lateness)
- 'Accidentally' damaging something to which the other person is deeply attached
- Being really slow when you know the other person is in a hurry

Below-the-belt attacks

This form of attack goes for the exact things the other person dislikes about themselves, feels vulnerable about or ashamed of, such as the shape of their nose, their goofy teeth, their breath, their difficulties in lovemaking, etc. The following justifications are often used in the face of such attacks:

- 'You should be grateful for my honesty. I'm only telling you what others wouldn't dare.'
- 'It's best we're straight with each other.'
- 'I need to feel I can be honest with you without you always doing that hurt little boy number.'

Threatening to leave

Threatening to leave or making an exit without saying when or even whether you're coming back can be particularly vicious. It can trigger extremely painful infantile feelings of abandonment in the one who is left. Cutting off by leaving means cutting off the possibility of communication, understanding and resolution. It is an entirely different thing to say 'I just need some breathing space. I'll be back in x hours.' This reassures the frightened inner child in the other person that you are not gone forever and will be coming back.

Odious comparisons

An unfavourable comparison is made to the other person directly or indirectly, e.g. referring to how good-looking X is, how youthful or clever Y is, or how very caring Z is. This is often disguised as a casual remark to make it seem harmless. Common justifications include such sentiments as, 'I was only making a simple remark', 'Everyone else says the same thing about X and Y', or 'I don't know why you're so touchy about it'.

■When anger moves to hate

> *'The Dormouse is asleep again', said the Hatter, and he poured a little hot tea upon its nose.*

> (Lewis Carroll, 1856/2003)

The energy of hate is a slower, colder and more sustained energy, when compared with the quick hot rush of rage or anger. Hate has time on its side from all the turning over in one's mind of bitter thoughts, stored-up disappointments and unexpressed hurt. It is analogous to ivy, which starts out slowly and is quite pretty, but before long has taken hold and entwines itself around anything that is living, throttling its capacity to breathe and flourish. In anger or rage there is a 'moving towards'. In hate, there is no moving towards, rather a sense that 'I hold you in too much contempt to want to share my anger with you. I have no wish to resolve anything. It's gone too far now.'

Some people are quite oblivious to the fact that they feel hatred towards someone in their life, but to any emotionally aware onlooker it is obvious.

■Childhood origins of destructive/damaging relationships in the present. From loving in torment as a child to tormented loving in adulthood

Loving in torment in parent – child relationships often perpetuates itself in terms of the child then loving in torment in later life. Loving in torment means that the child did not feel safe in their parents' love. They may have felt that they could easily lose that love, that the emotional bond with the parent is fragile or precarious. Or they may have felt that their parents' love could quickly turn into rejection or into something frightening, shaming or hating. All too often children with this experience move from hurt to hate, because it's far less painful.

From hurt in childhood to hate in adulthood

To hate somebody often means that you had at some time a deep need of them which has not been met. Indeed, destructive behavior can be fuelled by frustration of unmet childhood needs, which is still haunting the person on some level. These often include the frustrated need:

- to be acknowledged;
- to be loved;
- to be listened to;
- to be appreciated;
- to be understood;
- to be met with concern;
- to be respected.

When the person experiences this same need being frustrated in a relationship in later life, this can trigger all that childhood pain, but now without conscious awareness. Like a wounded animal, the person lashes out in the present because of these painful relationship experiences in their past. The person on the receiving end can end up paying not only for failing to meet their needs now, but also for those unmet childhood needs.

For example, in counselling, Jack, a forty-year-old man, realised that he was playing out in his personal relationships his anger about the rejection he had experienced in childhood. His mother had suffered from post-natal depression and, as a result, she found it difficult to have loving feelings towards Jack. To make matters worse, when Jack was nine he was sent away to school whilst his brother stayed with his mother. In adulthood, Jack left a very long trail of broken female hearts. He would love them, but his love would turn to indifference at best, or hate and disgust at worst. With his counsellor, he was able to get in touch with agonising feelings of hurt and anger towards his mother, which he had repressed for all those years. He realised that he was getting his revenge on her by doing to other women what he felt his mother had done to him. With new insight and after much grieving he finally loved in peace.

■From childhood victim to adult persecutor

As children we cannot leave home. For many children this means putting up with years of anger and criticism from the parental figure. Yet it can be dangerous to protest about this. The child needs the parent too much and cannot risk withdrawal of love. Alice Miller expresses this phenomenon well: 'Unable to leave, he must put up with everything; not until he has grown up can he take any action, avenge himself for his own misfortune' (Miller, 1987). In adulthood, however, often without conscious awareness, he may then discharge years of bottled-up anger and resentment.

In some families, vulnerable, warm or tender feelings are taboo. No one in the family models how to express hurt and no one shows empathy if hurt is expressed. So when feeling sad, hurt or disappointed, family members will just get angry instead. As one nine-year-old from such a family said, 'When I am sad, I just go out and kick something'. This is the legacy that is taken into personal relationships in later life, namely an internal working model of a relationship where it is not safe to say, 'I feel hurt' or 'I am sorry', etc. Rather they only know how to defend themselves from having these feelings in the first place.

■Childhood origins of being drawn to people who are unkind, angry and attacking

Some people seem attracted to those who are abusive in some way, through put-downs, constant criticism or actual physical attack. They may leave and start a new relationship with someone whom they are convinced is different, only to find that after a while the attacks start all over again. They can't seem to break the pattern.

What is happening here is being locked into a negative repetition of what they experienced as a child in a harsh family culture. Completely unconsciously, in relationships in later life the person then takes on the role of submissive victim with the other person being the attacker (repeat of childhood).

This painful repeat of the past not only happens in adult intimate relationships, but it can also happen at work and when parents let their children and teenagers abuse them and treat them as doormats, slaves or punch bags.

Freud called such behaviour 'repetition compulsion'. This means the pull to repeat the past. He and others argue that this is the mind's way of trying to work something through in order to resolve it.

Evidence-based research now shows that unless people work through their original childhood relationship pain, they can replay these negative relational patterns to their grave (Lane et al., 2015).

In contrast people who have been treated with warmth and respect as a child and who have not felt frightened of their parents or other key adults such as teachers, are likely to have a quick and healthy response to signs that a relationship is becoming abusive or emotionally impoverished, and to know intuitively that they deserve far more than this. Sadly, people who have known too many destructive relational patterns in childhood often don't know this, and so stay in destructive relationships for far too long. They think this is how life is. They have no real concept of the joys of a tender, respectful, empathic and loving relationship.

■Love made envious

In some close relationships, it is envy that leads to destructive behaviour. Some people would like to think this only happens in childhood relationships in the form of sibling rivalry, but this is not the case. It can be very painful to see someone in your life being successful in some way and living a meaningful life, when your own life feels pretty empty or somewhat banal. In such situations, conscious and unconscious envy can come out in destructive attacks (in all manner of ways we've discussed), eating away at the other person's confidence. As Dostoevsky's 'idiot' Prince Myshkin said, because he could not forgive others their happiness, he must 'trample on the joy of others'.

Power over / power under / power with

■Objective

All too often in key relationships, there can be some form of abuse of power, albeit at times very subtle with one person using power over the other person in a destructive, hurtful way. This is not surprising, as for generations children have been disciplined at home and at school in ways that include some form of submission/dominance, e.g. frightening the child into compliance and obedience. Punishment and isolation rooms are still used in many schools today. So in a way, many of us have had training in submission/dominance modes of interaction.

It is all too easy for people to find themselves playing victim or persecutor roles in key relationships or alternating between the two. 'Power over' or dominant interactions can be found in nagging, controlling, criticising, put-downs and all manner of other forms of abuse. In contrast, when someone finds themselves in a submissive position, this can lead to feelings of impotence, helplessness, low self-esteem, being a doormat, etc. It can also lead to a buildup of hidden resentments over time, leading to feelings of rage and/or contempt, which are at some point acted out through some form of major destructive act to self or others.

This exercise aims to help people to become more aware of submission/dominance patterns in their relationships (past and present) as a key first step to shifting to more healthy modes of interaction or ending certain relationships whether the other person has some form of emotional investment in 'Power over'. The exercise is also to celebrate really good relationships in the participant's life (if they have some), which are represented in the 'Power with' drawings. 'Power with' relationships mean that both parties are relating in a way that enhances the lives of both parties. Many creative ventures are born of such relationships.

■Instructions to give the participant

Look at the drawings of 'Power over', 'Power under' and 'Power with' patterns of relating. Tick or colour in the figures that represent you in some of the key relationships you have had in your life past or present. Then, if you like, write the name of the person next to the figures. If some of the power over/under relationships you have experienced are not in the drawing, draw them in the empty circles. Now move to the 'Power with' drawings. As before, if any of these lovely relationship scenes feel familiar, tick them or colour them in. Now stand back and look at what you have written/drawn.

What have you learned? Is someone's name coming up more than once? Are you more often the dominant one in the relationship, the submissive one, or a mixture of both? Or have you played different roles in different relationships? Are you in more 'Power with' relationships today than in your past, and less 'Power over'/'Power under' ones?

If you are still in too many 'Power over' or 'Power under' relationships today, what can you do to change things? How can you be with people you know and/or choose people in the future to ensure that for more of the time you enjoy 'Power with' interactions? If you repeatedly find yourself being submissive or dominant in your relationships, think about what you are unconsciously playing out from painful relationships in your past. If you feel stuck in this form of relating (you've been doing it for years), counselling or psychotherapy would be a good thing to consider, too.

■Development – Power replays from childhood

Ask the participant to look at their childhood experience of submission/dominance modes of relating at school and at home. Using sandplay miniatures, drawing or clay, ask the participant to depict relationships in their childhood or adolescence when they were in a submissive position, and an adult (e.g.

teacher/parent/bully/relative) was abusing power. Ask the participant to write what they would want to say to that person now.

From doing the exercise, if the participant seems interested in the notion of repetition compulsion (Freud), and how they, or the person they have that key relationship with, may be replaying submission/dominance modelled from childhood, you might like to explain the psychoanalytic term 'identification with the aggressor'. This means that, even despite our best intentions, we can treat someone else in the negative ways we were treated or saw someone else being treated. (e.g. watching domestic abuse). In other words, we bully as we have been bullied (or seen bullying), control as we have been controlled (or seen control). It is often only as a result of working through our feelings about the original 'persecutor' that we can stop doing this and/or move away and on to a healthy relationship without an abuse of power.

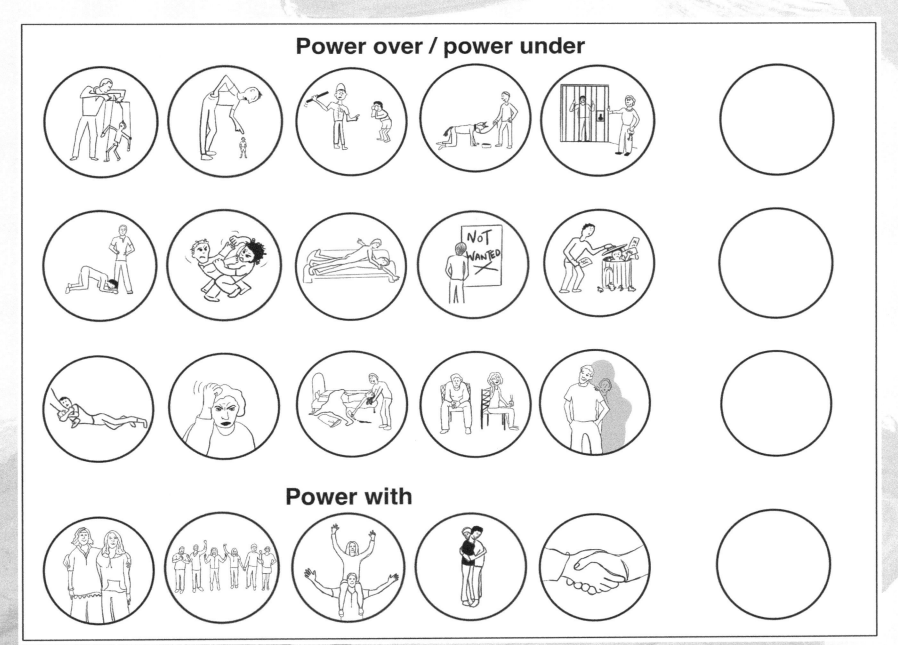

Figure 5.1

Toxic shame

■Objective

Shame is a very powerful and painful emotion. It is experienced by the body-mind as an assault on the self. Neuroscience research shows that feeling shame activates an immune system response of increased pro-inflammatory cytokines and cortisol (the same chemical reaction when you have experienced a physical wound and immune cells rush to the wound and start to repair tissue). This is because your bodymind has registered the shame as an assault, but this time on the self, not on the body. The worrying thing is that excessive production of inflammatory cytokines contribute to inflammatory diseases, linked to heart problems, cancer and depression (Dickerson et al., 2004: meta-analytic review of 20 laboratory stressor studies).

Shaming events can also result in long-term negative core beliefs about the self as being worthless, rubbish, unimportant or intrinsically bad. Furthermore, when you have been shamed, there is always 'shame-rage' underneath. This is extreme and intense, a direct response to the acute sense of assault by the shamer on one's very personhood. Guilt is usually far easier to deal with as the criticism is about something you have done rather than your very personhood.

This exercise aims to enable the participant to appreciate that they do not have to remain passive in their response to shaming and discouragement and to re-visit shaming experiences of the past but this time with you as advocate to help them find their appropriate protest and anger. As Bar-Levav (1990) says: 'Anger helps us reassert our sense of power and maintain our dignity and self-respect'.

■Instructions to give the participant

Shaming events, particularly in childhood, are very powerful. Unless talked about with an empathic other, in order to modify their emotional charge, they can leave a legacy that is emotionally toxic and physically harmful.

People can suffer from all manner of long-term misery from unprocessed shaming experiences from their past, including feelings of defeat and hopelessness and, in particular, social avoidance or social phobias.

Think of times you've felt shamed, either recently or at some time in your past. What did it make you feel? If it helps I will say some words that people frequently feel when shamed. Just ignore the words that are not right and say yes (or press the buzzer) if correct. Here goes: *Frozen, a person without a voice, a nothing/nobody, worthless, rubbish, a sinner, very very alone.* What other words would you use? Which aspect of you did you feel the shamer attacked? Again, ignore the words that are not right and say yes (or press the buzzer) to the ones that do feel right. Here goes: *Your self-worth, your confidence, your intelligence, your courage, your social skills, your ability to stay no, some other aspect of yourself that you really value.*

With any shaming event, it's vital to detoxify your feelings by finding your healthy anger or protest about the event. If you didn't do so at the time, it's fine to do so later. A powerful statement now can be a powerful healing force. This is because vividly imagined action and the real action activates some of the same neural pathways in the brain. So draw or write in the box your protest/rage/anger at being treated in this way.

How do you feel now you've done this? If you would like to, stand up, imagine the shamer is sitting on that chair now and say these things to him/her.

■Development – Finding your 'no'. Finding your 'stop right there'

What to say to the participant: Shaming a child is always grossly unfair due to the power differential. Children have few or no emotional resources to stop this lethal attack on the self. They are too open and vulnerable. But you can symbolically find ways to protect that 'child in you' after the event, by finding health protest now. Finding your 'no' and boundaries now can be satisfied in part through creative or artistic expression, rather than suppressing the need or acting it out in real life.

Now ask the participant to make an image of a shamer, controller or bully from their life story in an art form (clay, sandplay, drawing). Taking their power back can then be carried out symbolically on the lump of clay, or on a drawing of the shamer with paint or words. It is also possible to safely express the intensity of shame-rage by using the art image as a container. This can prevent the feelings being played out destructively in other relationships (displacing feelings on to other people which actually relate to the original shamer). It also means that feelings do not have to be turned inwards against the self.

Some people worry that the participant (particularly a child/teenager) will enact the rage in real life, once it has been 'rehearsed' through the art image. But most children and adults totally understand the difference between symbolic play and what is acceptable in the outside world. Children should be given a clear explanation of the boundaries of the experience. That said, if you are in any doubt as to the participant's ability to understand the distinction between symbolic play and reality, don't do the exercise.

Toxic shame

Figure 5.2

Managing conflict badly

■Objective

So many people have no adult models from childhood of how to communicate anger and resentment in appropriate and healthy ways that bring about resolution, not blame. This can leave people in later life communicating their anger through destructive means and/or turning their anger against the self. This exercise is therefore designed to enable participants to consider how they may be unintentionally spoiling their relationships through: (a) a buildup of unspoken resentment, anger, hurt or hate; and (b) a lack of relational resources in terms of negotiation and conflict resolution skills. This is with the hope that the participant can then move forward and use healthier ways of interacting in times of stress and conflict.

■Instructions to give the participant

If a significant relationship is to be emotionally healthy, it is vital to know how to express anger and resentment effectively in ways that leave both parties feeling all right. Without these skills, people can spoil their relationships with all manner of verbal attacks or other damaging ways of interacting. Sometimes the most lethal of these are covert, not overt. In the picture, look at the different forms of attack commonly used in significant relationships. Then think of key relationships in your life (past or present). Look at the picture. If there are forms of attack depicted there that you have used in a relationship, past or present, colour them in with a particular colour, tick them or mark with your initials. If there are forms of attack depicted in the picture that someone has used against you, use a different colour or mark or their initials or name. You might like to mark on the picture the negative interactions your parent/s used, too. There is a blank spot in case you want to draw a form of attack that has been part of your life but is not represented here.

Now stand back and look at what you have drawn. What do you feel? What have you learned? Which negative interaction have you marked more than once? What has it been like to have this sort of negative interaction in your life? How has it impacted on you as a person? Have you moved into doing to others what was done to you in childhood?

Are you with someone who is treating you as you were treated in childhood, with similar forms of attack? Freud called this 'repetition compulsion', meaning the way that a person unconsciously repeats aspects of their painful past as a means of trying to come to terms with it.

Is there anything you might like to do/say/change in your life as a result of what you have learnt from doing this exercise?

■Development – Moving from negative to positive ways of managing conflict

If the participant has realised that he or she has had no models of healthy conflict resolution, it may be appropriate to move to Chapter 7 – 'Tools and techniques to improve and repair relationships' – and use some of the information there as psycho-education for the participant to take away as homework to try to do next time there is a conflict in a key relationship in their life.

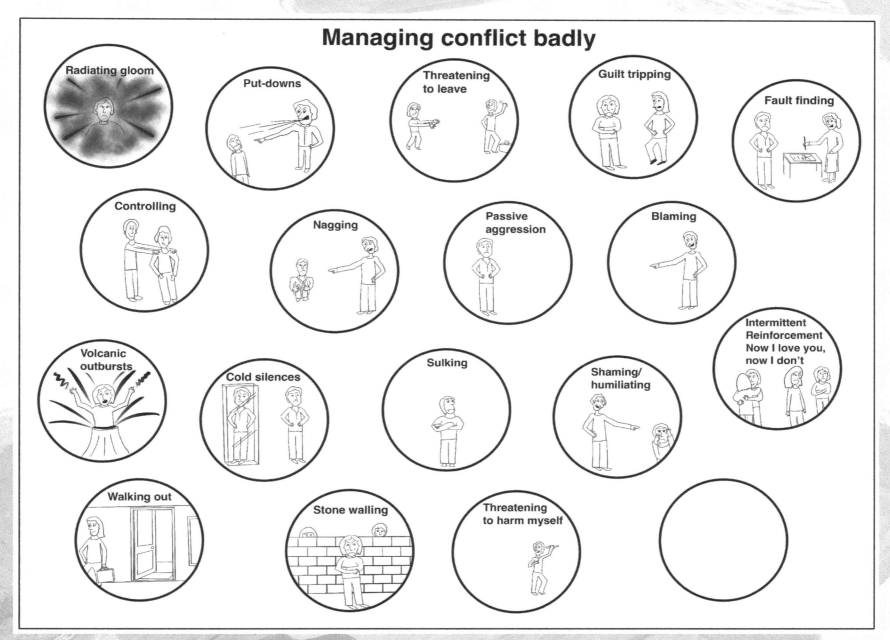

Figure 5.3

Controlled

■Objective

It is too easy for people to disregard or play down bad treatment in a relationship as 'something that just happens', or to pretend to themselves and others that it really isn't that bad. The objective of this exercise is therefore to focus on these oppressive aspects of a relationship, as heightened awareness is a vital step to change.

This exercise is for people who have let themselves be controlled or bossed about in their relationships (at home, work or school) and don't have a repertoire of how to react differently and to find their 'no'. The exercise aims to heighten the participant's awareness of control issues in key relationships in their life. It is also designed to empower them to think of new options. It is hoped that the exercise will also help them to address what happened in childhood that led them to allow themselves to be controlled today. Finally, it is hoped they find their empowered anger. When someone moves into obedience and compliance, there is always some underlying rage, even if the person is not in touch with this. This is because mammals (including humans) are genetically programmed to feel rage when their freedom is restricted (Panksepp, 2004). It may be very useful for the participant to access this rage. Then through having these strong feelings acknowledged and heard by you, hopefully they can be helped by you to transform the rage into empowered anger and find the words to say it in ways that can be heard.

■Instructions to give the participant

Think of all people in your life, past and present, you have felt controlled by. Go right back to childhood in your mind. During the controlling times you may have felt you shrunk, become a smaller, tighter version of yourself, lost your self-respect, flair, expansiveness, potency, and felt depressed, dulled or the opposite – enraged.

Think what you felt at the time. Write what your feelings were in the 'Feelings' oblong in the picture.

Now look at the 'You will . . . ' unfinished sentences. Write what you felt were the most powerful psychological messages from all the controlling people, e.g. 'You will be perfect', 'You will be what I want you to be' and 'You will not do anything I disapprove of'.

Now stand back from the picture. How has your life been impacted by having your freedom restricted in these ways? It is important to find your empowered anger, your 'no', so that you can stop being controlled by people in your present or future. So, describe what you feel like doing to people in your life who have tried to control you, boss you about or bully you. Write this on the controlling hand if you like or on a separate piece of paper big enough to hold all your feelings of rage or anger.

In terms of your over-compliance, unthinking obedience or letting yourself be controlled in relationships today, what from your childhood relationships do you think you are still replaying in these 'Power over' relationships today? How can you support yourself in future to be more assertive and stop yourself being controlled? How can you creatively channel your angry feeling about being controlled, so that you set clearer boundaries with people and find your natural assertive 'no' and 'stop'?

■Development – Coercive control

If this exercise has truly engaged the participant in terms of them saying it has been or is still a huge part of their life, it may be worth looking at the various aspects of coercive control. The UK government recently introduced a new domestic abuse offence of 'coercive and controlling behaviour', carrying a penalty of up to five years in prison as well as a fine. This is because the impact can be so psychologically damaging.

If this is relevant to the participant who wants to look at whether coercive control is part of a current relationship, then read out the various forms of coercive control to see if she or he can relate to them:

- *Unreasonable demands* and threats if you don't agree with these demands: 'You must do what I want you to do', which can include having sex; 'You must wear that dress, not the other one'; 'You must have the meal ready on the table for me when I come in'; and 'You can't eat that food'.
- *Put-downs, contemptuous name-calling, shaming, humiliating*, sometimes in front of friends, as ways to make you feel awful about yourself.
- *Restriction of what you can and can't do*, e.g. you can't meet that family member or that friend, when you are allowed out, etc.
- *Control over spending.* Looking at what you are spending and telling you want you can and can't buy (even when it's your own money).
- *Controlling your use of phone, tablets, social media accounts, etc*. Changing passwords, saying when you can use them and not, and who you can and can't speak to.
- *Destruction of things which are valued.* Examples include possessions, photos emails and text messages.

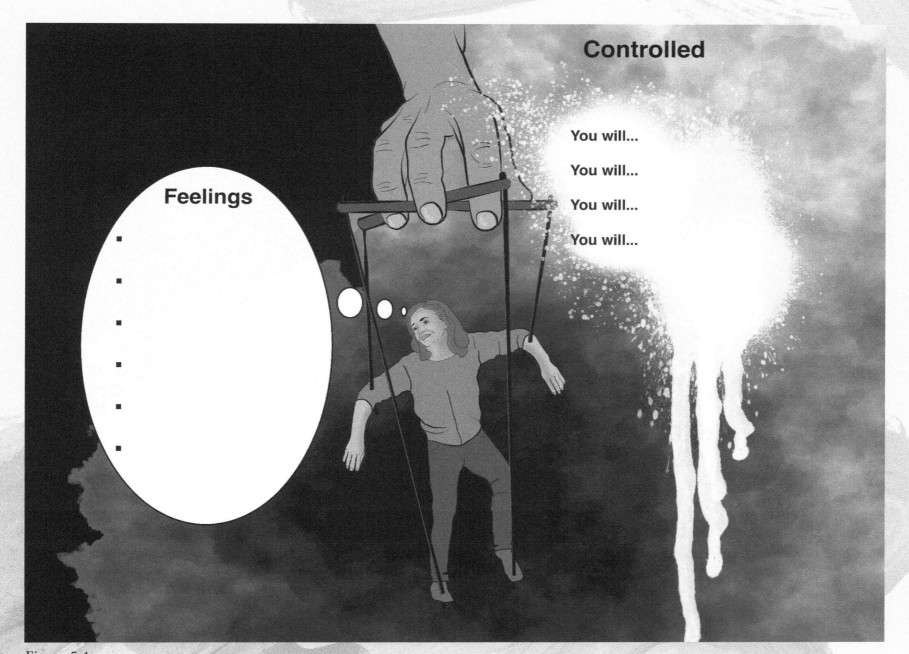

Figure 5.4

Emotional baggage

■Objective

This exercise is about the intergenerational transmission of misery. When a parent or other significant adult in a child's life has suffered considerable emotional pain, loss or trauma and doesn't get help to work through these feeling, (namely get therapy or counselling), the child can be deeply affected.

Despite their very best efforts and intentions, parents do pass on aspects of their own misery, unfinished business, and neuroses to their children. This can happen from generation to generation. Even the neonate has been shown to have the same brain chemical profile (decreased positive arousal chemicals and increased stress hormones) as those of his/her mother, when the mother was depressed or very anxious in pregnancy. In fact, parents who are anxious or depressed in pregnancy (and don't get help) are shown to have a negative impact on their children's mental and physical health, right up to and including the teenage years (Field et al., 2017a;b) It only takes one person to break the cycle of the intergenerational transmission of misery by getting help, in pregnancy, or at any other time during the child's life.

When a person is burdened with emotional baggage that belongs to someone else, it is vital that this is talked about with an empathic other, so that they can stop carrying that baggage around with them day in, day out, which costs too much in terms of quality of life. This exercise therefore offers an important way to think about emotional baggage, so that it starts to lose some of its power. As a result of this exercise, the participant may need support and encouragement to go into counselling or therapy to work through and grieve over particularly painful aspects of their emotional baggage.

■Instructions to give to participants

This exercise is to enable you to consider how you may be carrying out emotional baggage from your past, which actually belongs to

someone else! Here are some examples: thinking your loved ones will always reject you, because you felt rejected by your father because he was rejected by his father; being anxious and frightened because your mother was anxious and frightened; being afraid to make mistakes because you had a very strict teacher who would only accept 'perfect'.

Part one

Consider which aspects of your emotional baggage actually belong to someone you have known, and which you've ended up carrying in your own life in some way (meaning being deeply affected by it). Write these in the various spaces of the 'Emotional baggage' in the picture. Here are some things other people who did the exercise realised they were carrying: their parent's negativity and moaning, their parent's anxiety, depression, low self-esteem, anger, closed beliefs of what is right and proper, closed attitude to money/sex/power/success, their parent's prejudices, and their teacher's need for perfection and intolerance of even the smallest mistake.

Look at what you have written. How does it make you feel knowing you have been carrying these things that actually belong to other people? Think how you could now put down the baggage you have been carrying and which will be easier to put down and which harder.

Part two – Breaking free from emotional baggage

Write on a separate piece of paper the aspects of you that have not been blighted by someone else's emotional baggage and that are very different traits to those of significant adults in your childhood who contributed to your emotional baggage. You might write, for example: 'I am not anxious, I am not depressed. I can take risks. I can explore.' Congratulate yourself on these! You might like to light a candle and put it beside these aspects of self that are clearly you, not them, and which are deeply valued aspects of who you are.

■ **Development – Positive intergenerational transmission**

Ask the participant to consider positive intergenerational transmission. Ask them therefore to draw or write down the good things that have been passed down to them from their parents (e.g. particular family traits/qualities).

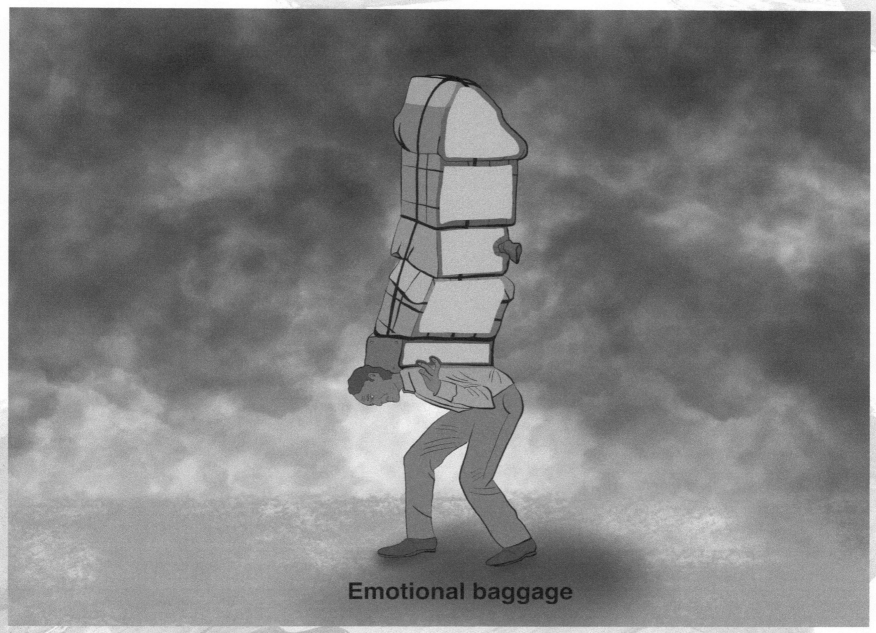

Emotional baggage

Figure 5.5

Hidden resentments

■Objective

If conflict avoidance becomes the norm in a relationship, it often irrevocably damages a relationship. It can be reduced to a 'shell' of itself as unspoken resentments block loving, warm feelings. In a sexual relationship, unspoken resentments often kill off sex. Moreover, if conflict is avoided both parties learn nothing about what the other person feels, needs or simply can't stand, and so the relationship cannot really move on and develop. Some conflict-avoiding relationships become banal or superficial, others are blighted by stone-walling and cold silences, others become marred by bitterness and contempt. Many relationships die as a result.

This exercise offers a way of looking in a detailed way at the cost of hidden resentments to a relationship that the participant cares about. It is also hoped that participants will address why expressing resentments instead of bottling them up feels so dangerous, or anxiety provoking, and offer ways forward for better relational health.

■Instructions to give participants

Think of people in your past or present towards whom you hold resentments that have never been expressed. On a separate zigzag for each person write their name in the picture and then a sentence beginning 'I resent . . .'.

Look at all the resentments and the people's names. Looking back on it, was it right you never voiced these resentments because you thought they were too fragile or would have exploded into rage, or are there any people in your picture to whom you wish you had found a way to express what you truly felt but were too anxious to do so?

Research shows that conflict avoidance damages relationships and stops them from growing, but in some relationships, it is necessary because of a person's volatility.

Have you had any good role models of handling conflict well or have you witnessed too many examples of conflict being handled badly through screaming, shouting, sulking or stone-walling which has made you fear conflict?

Think of a valued relationship in your life now. Do you have hidden resentments? Are you blocking this relationship from developing and deepening by not finding a good way to say these things in reality? Is the effect of leaving these things unsaid adding to your stress levels? Are you too anxious to voice them? Or do you think you are right in believing that the person for whom you feel these things is too emotionally fragile, volatile or cut off from what they feel, to be able to hear these things and benefit from them? There is a reality with some people in some circumstances of 'hitting people with honesty'. Hence at times lack of authenticity and openness may be appropriate. If this is not the case, would you like instead to dare to address conflict well with that person? What do you need to say, do or discuss together? How will you say it? What help do you need to do this?

■Development – Help for good conflict management

If the participant has had no really good models of healthy conflict management, you could support them now with rehearsal of some key ways of safely addressing resentments in a relationship. The best thing is to study the following techniques in Chapter 7 of this book and in particular the 'When you . . . I feel' exercise and the 'Like/don't like' game. Explain to the participant how these work.

Ask them to imagine that the person to whom they hold resentments is in the room and ask them to try out voicing the resentments. Help the participant if their tone is still critical and 'blamey'! Appreciate when they do it really well with strength and calm. Ask them, 'How do you feel having done this? Have you stated your needs clearly enough?' Ask them to consider whether they think the person to whom they want to voice the resentments will be up for doing the exercise . . . That is important, too, in making the decision as to whether to do this in reality!

Figure 5.6

So many difficult/annoying people in my life

■Objectives

All of us have known difficult, annoying and/or downright cruel people in our lives. Sometimes such people bring us down and they feel like they haunt our lives, in actuality or, if now a part of our past, in our minds. Other difficult people we navigate well and manage with all manner of social skills to move on from, so that these people no longer mar our quality of life. Such people are a key aspect of anyone's life story so need to be talked about and shared with a listening other. The clever or thoughtful management of difficult people we have known needs to be celebrated. Those who continue to haunt us, or have other negative effects, need also to be thought and felt about and discussed in terms of how they can be better managed (in terms of their negative place in the participant's mind or if they are still in their life now).

■Instructions to give the participant

Think of people in your past or present who have made your life difficult or downright painful. Write their names on the white lines. If they have been extremely difficult/painful, write them in very large letters. If they have been difficult/painful but not in a significant way, write their names smaller. Treat the picture as graffiti – just keep adding more names until you think you have got them all down there. Don't worry if there are a lot of names. Remember to think of childhood, teenage years and adulthood.

Now look at what you have written. What do you feel seeing all their names together? Who is still negatively impacting you today, in your mind and/or in reality? What are you proud of in terms of how you managed/navigated some of these people's hurtful or difficult behavior? Which peo-

ple would you have liked to have treated/navigated differently? If they were here now, what would you say to them?

What do you want to do with them on the picture? You can write something next to their name or scribble on them. Talking with someone who understands about the pain/'agro' these people have caused you also means they can have less power in your mind.

■Development – The gallery of sculptured difficult people (group exercise)

A fun, safe but powerful exercise to do in a group follows. Ask the group to pair up, and to label themselves person A and person B. In each pair, person A will pretend person B is a lump of clay and then mould them into someone in their past or present who was/is difficult/annoying/cruel, etc. Person B must cooperate and hold the pose given to them (like a statue). Person A then trains person B in one or two of the difficult people's statements and gestures. Then all the sculptors move away, leaving the gallery of difficult people. Declare the gallery open! In the order they choose, all the sculptors (persons A) are asked to visit each exhibit in turn, including their own. When they pull an imaginary string at the back of each of the sculptures, the difficult people statues begin to speak and use the gestures they have been trained to do. Persons A can respond and take their power back in any way they like (but no physical attacks of course). They can tell the difficult people statue to shut up or say whatever they like. After a while, with a drum or equivalent (otherwise you won't be heard because it gets loud), declare the gallery closed. This means persons A are asked to move to the sides of the room. Dim the lights if you can. Talk the sculptures through what happens next and ask them to enact what you say. 'In the middle of the night, the sculptures come alive and start being difficult with each other. They get increasingly difficult until eventually they explode and go into a meltdown ending as a pool of treacle on the floor.' Persons A clap loudly. Switch roles and repeat the exercise.

Sit the group down and allow time for them to talk about what they felt. In particular, focus on how they felt, taking back their power in responding as they did to their difficult person in the exercise.

Figure 5.7

Anger fuelled by pain from the past

■Objective

This exercise is to help participants to distinguish their here-and-now anger from unresolved anger from their past: meaning anger from major life event/s which left considerable pain and hurt and which has never been properly worked through or talked about. This is known as archaic anger. Such feelings do not just go away, however much they are denied or suppressed. As Freud said, they just 'proliferate in the dark'. It is helpful to explain to participants some key points about archaic anger, in particular the following:

- Archaic anger is anger that is being expressed to someone in the present which really belongs to someone in your past, often a parent figure.
- Archaic anger feels primitive and intense because it is unworked through and years of being stored up inside, unspoken about, add to its intensity.
- Archaic anger is usually identified by the intensity and volume of your reaction to something that other people would have a far milder, low-key response.
- Archaic anger risks blasting people away from you. Some relationships are destroyed by these blasts.

■Instructions to give participants

When someone does something annoying and you feel rage rather than just irritation, then you may be experiencing archaic anger. This means anger still bottled up inside you from some painful relationship experience in the past. Think of a relatively recent incident involving someone else or a painful row or moment of conflict that you can remember clearly. It was of particular significance for you, although you may not quite know why. Now look at the tables below entitled 'Anger fuelled by pain of the past' and 'Healthy here and now anger'. Tick any of the statements in both lists that describe how you felt during or after the conflict. Now look at the table with the most ticks. This should help to inform you if in this row or moment of conflict your anger was mostly pain from your past, played out in the present, or healthy here and now anger. If it was past pain (archaic anger), talk through the memories that you think are fuelling your painful overreactions today.

■Development

Discuss with the participant how on future occasions they could support themselves better by informing a trusted intimate or other person when they think they might move or have moved into archaic anger (unresolved anger from the past). The concepts of foresight, mid-sight and hindsight can be very helpful here.

Example

Foresight: 'What I am going to say might seem somewhat irrational, because I think this whole issue has triggered a painful memory for me'. This alerts the other person to the fact that there may be a lot of childhood rage/hurt coming their way, and not to take it all personally.

Mid-sight: Hey, I'm sorry. I guess I'm shouting now because I've probably triggered something here which is probably not to do with you.'

Hindsight: Look, I've come to say I'm sorry. When I thought about what I said to you, I felt awful. I was being over the top. I think what I said to you wasn't actually about you. It was my angry feelings towards my mother for leaving me.'

Of course, foresight is best, but mid-sight is also very socially intelligent, and hindsight can heal so much in a relationship, too.

Table 5.1

Healthy here and now anger

	Tick box
The focus is on the resolution of the problem not on the desire to hurt A sense of 'We have a problem here, so how can we resolve it?' This is completely different in tone and energy to 'You are to blame because.', 'It's all your fault . . . '	
Owning your part in things/Willingness to look at what you contributed to this conflict The opposite of 'There is a problem but it's nothing to do with me'	
Healthy anger is vibrant, active and over Often known as 'warm anger'. There is a 'clean' feel to it, although it can still be loud and passionate.	
Ordinary rather than extreme expressions and notions about the other The other person makes you angry, frustrated, irritated, annoyed, rather than the extremes of archaic anger e.g. seeing the offending other as evil/an abuser/totally rotten/a psychopath.	
No vindictiveness, sadism or vengeful purpose	
Healthy anger is finite, communicated clearly and effectively, and so you can move on. No holding grudges, rather a quick regaining of the status quo	
Rows, conflicts and arguments do not feel catastrophic or dangerous, just a normal part of life	
Healthy anger leaves you feeling OK about yourself and the other person	

Anger fuelled by pain from the past

	Tick box
Raw intensity of response The event has triggered in you raw, unprocessed feelings of hurt, rage, shame, betrayal etc. from your past.	
A preoccupation with revenge You have a strong desire to make the other person feel what they have made you feel, or worse.	
A desire to hurt . . .with actions and/or words.	
Rumination: the same angry, indignant thoughts going round and round in your head You are preoccupied by what happened, and can't seem to let it go and move on. In-depth 'post-mortem' examination of the event: what you could have said or done.	
Negative responses to any apology or the attempts by the other person to make amends This is because the pull inside you is to punish not resolve. This is often due to an out of conscious awareness desire to punish this person for old hurts caused by people in your past	
Underlying deep sense of hurt Under all the anger, a deep hurt has been re-triggered from painful relationships in your past, e.g. times in your past when you were rejected, discouraged, shamed or humiliated, too unhelped. (Again often out of conscious awareness)	
Relief at having a core negative belief about yourself or others confirmed E.g. 'See, this proves how unlovable I am', 'See, this proves that you can't ever really trust anyone', 'See, this proves that everyone is really out to get me'.	

Further reading

Dickerson, S., Gruenewald, T. and Kernenv, M. (2004) When the social self is threatened: Shame, physiology, and health. *Journal of Personality*, December.

Field, T. (2017a) Prenatal anxiety effects: A review. *Infant Behav. Dev.*, November, 49: 120–128.

Field, T. (2017b) Prenatal depression risk factors, developmental effects and interventions: A review. *J. Pregnancy Child Health*, February, 4(1): 301.

Gottman, J. (2012) Four Negative Patterns that Predict Divorce (Parts 1 and 2). Accessed at: www.youtube.com/watch?v=FJDN3PKZ1KE; and www.youtube.com/watch?v=o5OdpPodpNY.

Jaremka, L., Glaser, R., Malarkey, W. and Kiecolt-Glaser, J. (2013) Marital distress prospectively predicts poorer cellular immune function. *Psychoneuroendocrinology*, November, 38(11): 2713–2719.

Lane, R. D., Ryan, L., Nadel, L. and Greenberg, L. (2015) Memory reconsolidation, emotional arousal and the process of change in psychotherapy: New insights from brain science. *Behav. Brain Sci.*, January, 38.

Relationships and fear

■About this chapter

> *To fear love is to fear life, and those who fear life are already three parts dead.*

> (Bertrand Russell, 1929)

The exercises in this chapter are designed for those people for whom intimate relationships are a huge challenge because of underlying, often crippling fears. Many times, people don't even know that the way they are acting in relationships which is causing themselves so much pain (as well as pain for their partners) is fuelled by fear. However, if such a fear is named, addressed, talked about and worked through with someone who understands the psychology of intimate relationship, then that fear can be modified to the point that it no longer blights someone's relationship life. The fear can then be managed rather than acted out. The exercises will support this process of naming fears, heightening awareness and supporting the participant to make informed decisions as to how to manage their fears well.

■Essential theory

The two key fears that can (if unaddressed) blight intimate relationships are fear of closeness/intimacy and fear of distance.

■Fear of intimacy

Many people fear intimacy. For adults, this can mean a preference for short-term relationships, one-night stands or multiple partners, as these may feel far safer than long-term, committed relationships. In other words, some people can tolerate intimacy for short, intense relating periods but run scared when a relationship threatens to develop. Other people fear intimacy in any form. Yet, we are genetically programmed to need people and to form attachment bonds, so trying to fight against this always comes at a price. The outcome is often a deep sense of meaninglessness at some time in life, a sense of futility or emptiness. Moore puts it beautifully: 'The unintimate person hovers nervously in air, separated both from her own depth and from the souls of others' (Moore, 1994b).

Other people who are frightened of intimacy may tolerate long-term relationships, providing they control the relationship. They do this by such things as limiting times of real closeness, staying within a safe range of emotions or making sure they get long periods of time apart. To quote Giovacchini, who describes one of his intimacy phobic patients: 'He was married, but his marriage seemed as barren as the iceberg and the space capsule. He described many situations in which he felt that any overture, no matter how tentative, made towards him was an intrusion.' (Giovacchini, 1989)

For some people, intimacy is experienced as such a threat to the self that any period of closeness has to be balanced with a period of withdrawal. Sometimes this is achieved by engineering sudden shifts from closeness to distance, e.g. 'I must be going now because I need to do *x*', or provoking a conflict in some way to sever the closeness. The person who fears intimacy may not know why he or she has such a strong impulse to withdraw after periods of closeness.

Fears of intimacy can spoil some of the richest experiences available to humankind, e.g. a deepening love in a long-term committed relationship, profound times of intense connection, or making love as opposed to just having sex. Furthermore, being in a loving relationship with someone who has a fear of intimacy can of course be extremely painful and emotionally depriving. The recipient can suffer all manner of rejections, withdrawals and long periods of isolation. It takes a strong and psychologically aware person not to take these things personally, and rather understand them as the avoidance needs of an 'intimacy-phobe'.

Sexual intimacy, an even greater threat

> *A great many [Casanovas] are uncomfortable immediately after sex; they don't know what to do or how to feel in the post-coital hush. One man said, 'the moment my penis goes down, my thoughts come back. And what they tell me is, "Let's get the hell out of here, buddy".'*

> (Trachtenberg, 1988)

For some people, when being loved feels suffocating, physical and sexual intimacy can hold even greater fears. This can lead to what is commonly known as a 'heart/genital split', where people cannot have loving and sexual feelings at the same time. So, for example, by being quick, matter of fact or rough in bed, a frightened person can give their partner the clear message of 'Look, I'll have sex with you, as long as no tender, loving feelings come in here too'. Some will make love and immediately find an excuse (often highly unconscious) to leave the bed. Doing so becomes a survival issue. Others, when they start to feel deeply loving toward their partner, may find themselves losing their sexual desire.

Childhood origins of fear of intimacy
A fear of intimacy often has its origins in some form of 'loving in torment' in one or more significant childhood relationships, a torment that leaves a child in fear of close relationships. Here are some origins.

Legacy of needy parental love
As the child grows up, the parent's needs, not the child's, start to become foreground in their relationship. The parent uses the child as a substitute partner, parent or confidante. Such needy parents are often not getting their needs met by their actual partners, friends or therapist. Some may still be carrying the pain of unmet needs from their own childhood. The unspoken messages from parent to child can be, 'I need you to love me, want me, adore me', 'I need you to make up for the love and attention I never got', 'I need you to help me to feel safe and good in the world' or 'I need you to take care of me'. This can leave the child feeling overwhelmed and/or inadequate and helpless at ever being able to satisfy, soothe or mend their needy, emotionally fragile or physically ill parent. Such a child is often referred to as the 'overburdened child' (Kohut and Wolf, 1978). The child becomes the parent's 'project' and so is the main vehicle for that parent's self-esteem. Once again, the pressure of this on the child can be great. With a frequently depressed, anxious, drunk or drugged parent, the child can feel that they are somehow drowning in their parent's negative mood states. They can also end up not being able to distinguish between their own feelings and those of their parent.

It is not surprising that when such a child reaches adulthood, he can experience as threatening those people who make demands of him. It can all too easily trigger the same feelings of impotence, fear and failure he had around his parent's needs. As one man who was frightened of intimacy in all his adult relationships said, 'I remember finding my mother's needs insatiable. I felt so inadequate, that I would never be able to satisfy them. I still have lots of drowning nightmares.' And so results long-term fear of intimacy.

Legacy of on–off parental love
When a child's natural instinct to love his parent is sometimes met well and at other times thwarted, fear of intimacy can result. The person may form a tragic connection in his mind between loving and rejection. Sometimes the most painful is the 'intermittent reinforcement' of a parent who 'blows hot and cold', loves one minute and not the next. This can be lethal as it excites hope. There can develop a basic mistrust in the other's love. Declarations of love can be viewed with suspicion as meaning, 'They don't really mean it', 'They'll only go off me soon', 'They must want something from me because it can't be me they want' or 'If I let people in they will only hurt or humiliate me'. And so results long-term fear of intimacy.

Legacy of controlling parental love
Here the parent may have been very loving, but also very controlling in the sense of making the child become as they want him or her to be. This can involve controlling the child to behave in a very compliant way, have certain feelings and not others, or even to have specific ambitions. Many people can be heard saying, 'My parents always wanted me to be a lawyer/doctor/accountant'. Sometimes wanting a child to succeed where they have not succeeded fuels this: 'I want them to do what I never did'. The child gives up their 'self' in order to become the person the parent wants them to be. Such parenting can leave a person in later life very wary of being controlled by others: 'If I let this person get close to me, they will only get me to be how they want me to be; I will lose me'. And so results long-term fear of intimacy.

Legacy of intrusive parental love

The intrusive parent is frequently unable to let their child just be, without fussing at him, watching and commenting on his every move, or telling him to do this or that. The child's body is cleaned, prodded, touched intrusively, e.g. nose wiped, hair straightened, clothes adjusted and perfected. In adolescence, the intrusiveness extends to the child's sexuality and personal life. As a result the child can feel endlessly monitored, admired and interfered with.

Not surprisingly, from this start in life, love in later life can trigger feelings of suffocation, intrusiveness and engulfment. Some people are aware that they fear intimacy because of how they were parented in childhood, but others are unaware of the connection.

■Fear of emotional distance and underlying fears of rejection/abandonment

Here are some statements made by people who live with fear of rejection or abandonment. The awful pain is very clear:

- 'When you look away, it's like you've gone away.'
- 'When we don't connect, it's as if you leave me in some awful desert.'
- 'When I feel she's losing interest in me, I end up doing some crazy things, like I'm possessed.'
- 'I was so afraid that he'd leave me, so I left him first.'
- 'In the end, everyone seems to go away.'
- 'When you are with me, I often think you don't want to be with me.'
- 'She'll leave me one day, I won't leave her.'

When people have ongoing fears of rejection or abandonment, they can be driven at times to desperate behaviour. Such behaviour may include all manner of clinging, rushing away, rushing towards, slamming doors, ultimatums, threats to leave, sleeping in the other room, pleading, begging, shouting, raging, extreme claims on the other person's time, and threats of or actual self-harm. The misery and self-loathing can be far-reaching. Furthermore, the fear of being left can build to such intensity that it may lead the person to paranoid acts such as spying on their partner, going through their possessions, following them, sitting

in the car outside their place of work, etc. During these times, they are desperate to re-establish a connection with their loved one, desperate to do anything that will help close the emotional gap, which can be experienced as being so big (even when it isn't in reality) that it is unbearable. When fears of rejection and abandonment are coupled with low self-worth, then desperate behaviour may also include:

- extreme self-sacrifice to gain the gratitude of the other person;
- always putting the other person's needs before their own;
- nourishing their partner in a hundred different ways, whilst leaving themselves emotionally starving.

If a person lives with persistent fears of being left, they can, entirely unconsciously, feed their partner the words to implant the idea of leaving. They may repeatedly say, 'You don't really love me, or want to be with me', 'I'm too boring for you really', 'You'll leave me one day, I won't leave you' or 'You're too good for someone like me'. Such statements repeated often enough over time can work like hypnosis. Others call it autosuggestion. Eventually the other person thinks, 'Maybe he's right – maybe I don't really love him. Maybe he really is unlovable, the way he's always implying he is.'

When a relationship is actually dying, fears of being left can lead to even more desperate behaviour, clinging and threats, controlling behavior in an attempt to stop the partner from leaving. All in all, when people are consumed by the fear of being left, they can experience all the emotional extremes and the frightening feeling storms of a small baby.

Childhood origins of fear of emotional distance (rejection/abandonment)

The person who has acute fears of being left may be unaware that their sometimes-desperate behaviour and angry attacks are usually an indication of unworked-through childhood or babyhood pain. In other words, they perceive the present through lenses coloured by unaddressed childhood pain.

Sadly, such a legacy of childhood pain can damage or destroy a relationship. It is annoying at best and infuriating and hurtful at worst to be on the receiving end of accusations of 'not being loving enough' day after day, when often there are no grounds in reality. Moreover, the person on the receiving end may be at a complete loss to understand the intensity of the repeated distress states and the barrage of accusations about their 'supposed' waning interest or failing love whenever they just pick up the newspaper, turn away fleetingly or momentarily look at an attractive person in the street. It can try the patience of most people and lead to feelings of being with a desperate child rather than an adult. Some people, feeling attacked, accused, pressurised, living on a totally unwanted and unwarranted rollercoaster day after day, may take their exit.

People say the past is past. This is exactly what it isn't. Painful memories, when not fully felt, thought about and worked through, live on to haunt us. Hence it is vital for a person to reflect on how they are playing out the past in their present.

Childhood abandonment and rejections that can haunt the person's relationship life in the present often comprise one or more of the following:

- Being left to cry as a baby when in need of comfort
- Separation anxiety that was left unsoothed/not taken seriously
- Being pushed away at the natural clingy stage
- Repeated failures of empathy and attunement
- Feeling of having lost one's beloved parent, or lost their love to the new baby, another sibling, parent's depression, alcoholism, etc.
- Having a parent whose love is on–off
- Painful long-term separations from a parent in childhood.

The irony is that when a parent is unable to deal with or even feel her child's distress states, it is often because when she herself was a child her own desperate states of need or longing were not acknowledged, tolerated or met with compassion by her parent/s.

■The fence sitters who fear both closeness and distance

He would emerge into social life for a brief foray in order to get a 'dose' of other people, but 'not an overdose'.

(Laing, 1967)

Some people are never comfortable for long either alone or in the company of a loved one. The famous psychoanalyst Harry Guntrip called these people 'fence sitters' because they are so uneasy with both isolation and intimacy and can never make a committed choice to either. Intimacy is desired, yet also feared. The 'fence sitters' engineer some alone time, but after a while feel lonely and yearn for togetherness. So they seek this out, but before very long, when reunited with their loved one or close friends, they feel claustrophobic and yearn for aloneness again. Then the whole cycle restarts. The milk-and-honey land of their own company, yearned for when in the company of others, fails to satisfy. The anticipation is always better than the actuality. The situation soon feels like self-imposed solitary confinement. And so it goes on and on with this restless to and fro. Here are some statements typical of this particular human torment:

- 'When I'm with people, I soon yearn to be on my own, and when I'm on my own I get lonely and want to be with people.'
- 'Sometimes I can only want to be with you by spending time away from you.'
- 'Whenever I'm not with her, I just yearn for her. But when I'm with her, I feel trapped.'

Fence sitters can leave a trail of confused, bewildered broken-hearted partners, some of whom can mistakenly take the other person's flights and avoidances as due to personal failings rather than understanding it for what it is. They may accuse the fence sitter of 'giving mixed messages' or 'blowing hot and cold', which is exactly right.

The first step to change is awareness. So it is hoped that the exercises in this chapter will support the participant to consider the two major underlying fears, which if not addressed often end perfectly good relationships.

When one partner has a fear of intimacy and the other has a fear of abandonment

It can seem like some kind of cruel fate that many people who fear closeness (intimacy) pair up with people who fear distance (rejection/abandonment). The common scenario goes like this: person A (fear of abandonment) complains about not having enough personal time with person B: 'You are never there for me' or 'I need more time with you'. Person B (fear of intimacy) complains, 'You always crowd me' or 'I need more time on my own'. The emotional withdrawal of person B leads person A (fear of abandonment) to pursue them. This makes person B (fear of intimacy) move even further away, feeling yet more threatened by the increasing neediness of their partner. Person A feels desperate and does desperate things. And so it goes on. Both people are in very primitive defence states of fight and flight. Neither of them may have any idea that the other is very scared, or of what, because neither says so. They may not even know themselves.

In summary, it is hoped that the exercises in this chapter will support awareness in such a way that people who are frightened of closeness will find their 'no' and their boundaries and be honest about their need for withdrawal time. As for the person who fears distance, it is hoped that through the raising awareness aspects of the exercises, they may start to separate out what is pain in the present from pain in their past and be able to hold back, wait and deal with their fears of abandonment with an empathic other, (perhaps you as facilitator) instead of acting out those fears in the relationship. The exercises in the final chapter of the book entitled 'Tools and techniques to improve and repair relationships' may also really help if you are seeing both people in the relationship together.

Fear of intimacy

■Objective

Fear of intimacy can lead to all forms of withdrawal, withholding and running away, which often bring abject misery to the people on the receiving end. Sometimes people are not aware that they have a fear of intimacy, or that they are moving into primitive flight mechanisms in an important relationship. This exercise is therefore designed to enable participants to consider whether their suspicions that they have a fear of intimacy are true, and if so what is fuelling their fear. If by doing the exercise they do feel they have a fear of intimacy, it is hoped that they can then develop more awareness of their flight and withdrawal reactions in personal relationships. From this they can learn to manage their fears in more creative ways and build up a wider range of relational resources and options that do not hurt themselves or their partners.

In the instruction section we refer to the different forms of parental love in childhood that can lead to fear of intimacy in adulthood. If the participant shows particular interest in these, you might like to read or relate what these are in more detail (see the theory section of this chapter).

Note

This exercise is only for those people who feel they have a fear of intimacy. Not everyone does, of course, so it would be pointless at best and very annoying at worst to ask someone who has a fear of abandonment and/or no fear of intimacy to undergo this exercise. So ascertain first whether this is felt to be an issue by the participant himself/herself.

■Instructions to give the participant

Look at the picture. Here are some of the underlying beliefs and feelings that fuel a person's fear of intimacy. Tick any of the images in the picture that you can relate to. If none of these apply to you, then draw your own. If you do have these fears, how might you deal with them in your relationships in the future in ways that are less hurtful to you and your partner?

You might like to think of any childhood experiences that could be fuelling your fears. Being a child who experiences one the following forms of parental love are common causes of fear of intimacy: needy parental love, on–off parental love, controlling parental love, intrusive parental love. Think also of childhood experiences of rejection, abandonment, separation, shaming, lack of respect for privacy, violations. If you are able to locate the origin, it's often the first step to changing and modifying your fears.

■Development – Finding your 'no'

The following quotation may be useful to discuss with the participant: 'Until he has a strong No in his repertoire he cannot have a strong Yes' (Resnick, 1993). This exercise will then help to empower the participant who fears intimacy with boundary-setting skills and with the ability to say 'no'. Suggest a role play. You play a 'needy demanding other' and ask the participant to practise putting down clear boundaries in a firm but non-angry way. Ask them to rehearse voicing their needs in terms of their current relationship: 'What I want is . . . ' (e.g. more time on my own); 'What I need is . . . '. (e.g. to have one hour every night on my own. I feel too suffocated without this. It's not personal. It's to do with what happened in childhood.)

The underlying message to the participant is that if they let other people get close, they can always negotiate and state their needs, e.g. for time apart rather than moving into primitive flight/withdrawal mechanisms which are very hurtful to the other person and can sometimes destroy good relationships.

Fear of intimacy

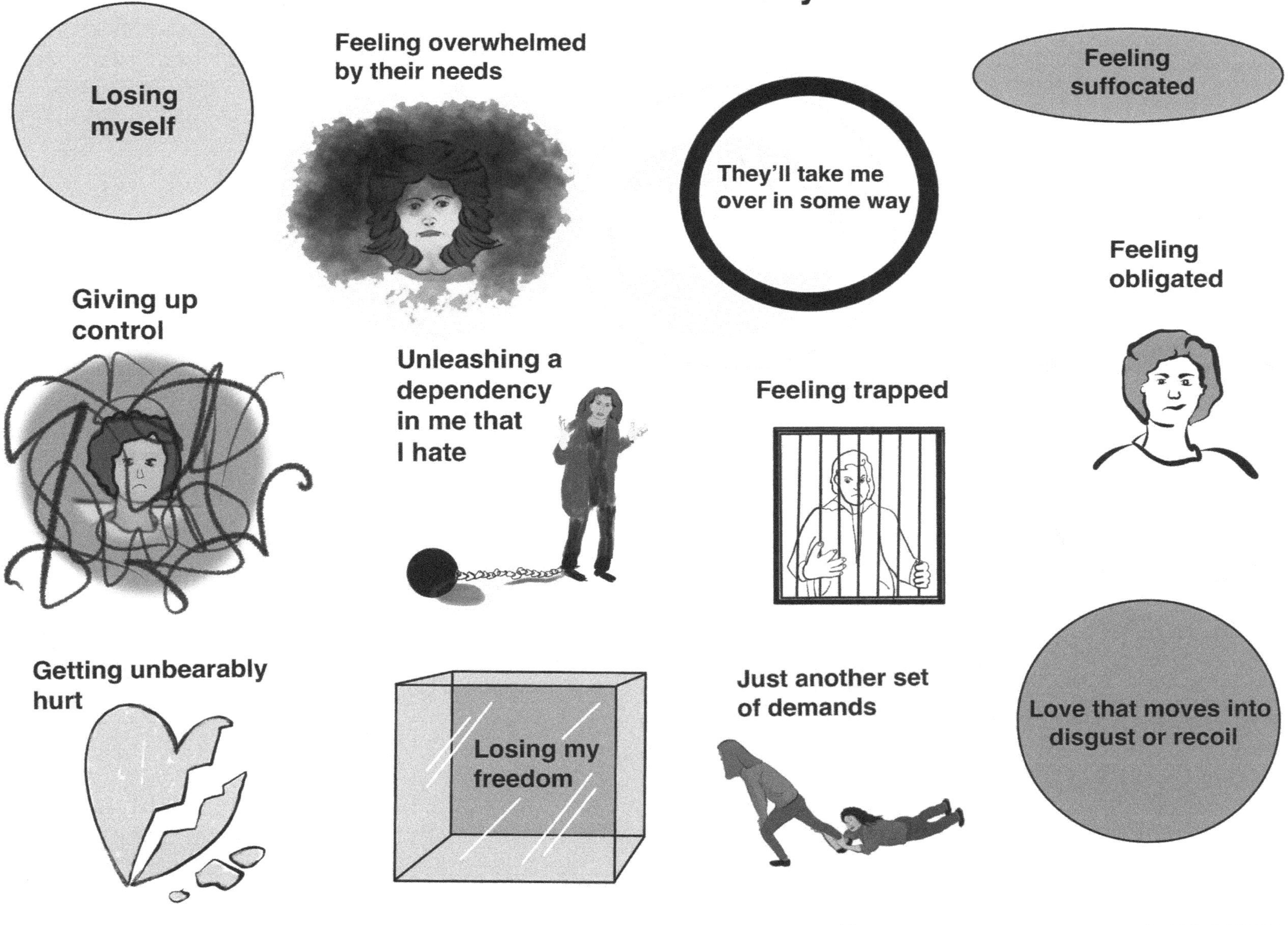

Losing myself

Feeling overwhelmed by their needs

They'll take me over in some way

Feeling suffocated

Giving up control

Unleashing a dependency in me that I hate

Feeling trapped

Feeling obligated

Getting unbearably hurt

Losing my freedom

Just another set of demands

Love that moves into disgust or recoil

Figure 6.1

Withdrawal, avoidance and leaving

■Objective

This exercise is for people who often use as withdrawal, avoidance, leaving as a form of protection in key relationships in their life. It is also for people who have been on the receiving end of someone else doing this to them.

Primitive fight /flight mechanisms deep in the old mammalian and reptilian part of our brains can be strongly activated in personal relationships. Sometimes, out of the blue, a person with a fear of intimacy and/or abandonment/ rejection says, 'I am leaving'. They can justify this to themselves with many excellent reasons as to why they need to go, whilst being oblivious to the factw that they are in the grip of a very primitive flight mechanism. Such fears are usually fuelled by memories of past experiences where someone has been intrusive, frightening or deeply hurtful in some way. When a person is haunted by their past in this way and has not addressed or worked through their emotional baggage, suddenly rushing away can feel like the only option. In that moment, staying feels impossible.

Other people act out their primitive flight mechanisms far more gradually. Over time, in their close relationships, they slowly withdraw quality attention, plans for a shared future, interest in the other's life, compliments, spontaneous gestures, presents, physical affection or meaningful conversation. It's like a picture in which the colour slowly fades. And then one day the person may actually leave – their relationship, by this stage, little more than an empty shell.

For other people, as soon as they have left, they feel bereft and so rush back. In other words, they experience two extreme sets of feelings in a short space of time – a desperate need to leave and then a desperate need to return. By whatever means the leaving is carried out, as the couple therapist Bob Resnick rightly says, 'Leaving is very primitive, it cuts off everything. It is a gross kind of veto power.' (Resnick, 1993) This exercise is therefore designed to help the participant to reflect on their flight mechanisms, the ones they have used in close relationships and the ones they have been on the receiving end of. The intention is to heighten awareness, and to motivate the participant to find far healthier ways of stating their needs and establishing boundaries in their personal relationships, instead of doing so by just leaving.

■Instructions to give the participant

When under stress in close relationships, one or both parties can move into primitive flight mechanisms. Some of these involve actual leavings, whilst others are 'leavings-whilst-staying', as in cold silences, sulking or withholding compliments, physical contact, love, etc. Look at the various flight modes in the picture. Tick the ones you use, or others have used against you. If other flight modes you use or have been used against you are not represented here, draw your own. If you are the person using these flight mechanisms, what is the fear underneath? What could you do differently instead of moving into flight or withdrawal?

If you are on the receiving end of someone else's flight mechanisms, what does it make you feel? What might you do differently next time it happens, so you don't feel so vulnerable, angry, hurt, etc.?

■Development – Looking at how to get your needs met without withdrawal/avoidance/leaving

Think of a particular time when you used a flight mechanism in a key relationship. Imagine you had stayed and used words, not flight. Try it now.

Fill in the end of these sentences:

- When you . . .
- I feel . . .
- So what I want is . . .
- Will you . . .?

What does it feel like to hear you being assertive in this way? Discuss the following quotation with the participant: 'some people don't know how to say No and stay. They only know how to say No by leaving.' (Resnick, 1993) Ask the participant to practise saying 'no' through role play so that they say 'no' in words rather than by leaving, sulking, etc. It may help to ask the participant to consider whether their sudden escapes or frightened leavings were in part due to a lack of modelling of negotiation, assertiveness and conflict resolution skills in their upbringing.

Withdrawal, avoidance and leaving

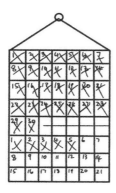

Time distance: I'm too busy to see you until.....

Sulking

A slow fading out of the relationship

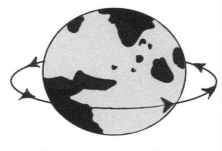

Geographical distance

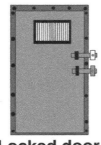

Locked door

Angry silence

Cold silence

A wall of work

I need some space

I must be going

Figure 6.2

Fears of closeness and fear of distance

■Objective

This exercise aims to enable the participant to become more aware of their own fears of closeness and distance in personal relationships. From a position of heightened awareness, it is hoped that they will then be able to address and manage their fears more effectively, resulting in far less pain for self and others.

Fears of intimacy and fears of emotional distance fuel many conflicts and much pain in personal relationships. Also, someone whose primary fear is intimacy often has an uncanny knack of entering into personal relationships with someone who fears emotional distance, and vice versa. If the two people do not address and work through their fears, their relationship can sometimes falter irrevocably. That said, some people yearn for closeness, and yet when they get it they become very frightened. Others yearn for separate time, and yet when they get it they feel lonely. Moreover, in one relationship the person's primary fear may be closeness, while in another it may be distance. We bring out different fears and hopes in each other. Hence this area is highly complex.

■Instructions to give the participant

Read through the two lists entitled 'Fear of intimacy' and 'Fear of emotional distance'. Both fears are extremely common and are often what trigger the most painful arguments in close relationships. This is particularly the case if neither party is aware of their underlying fears fuelling their angry attacks and criticisms.

Tick any of the statements on both lists that describe how you feel or have felt in important relationships, past or present. After completing this task see if you have more ticks on one list than the other. What is it like living with one of these fears or both of them? Or if you no longer have the fear at all or so intensely, what was it like living with the fear/s in the past? How do these fears spoil your relationships or have spoilt them in the past?

If you still have these fears, how might you be more creative around them in the future? How might you handle them better? If you keep suffering because of these fears, what stops you going into counselling or therapy for a period of time to address your pain once and for all?

■Development – Fears of loving or being loved

Ask the participant to draw the events in their life that they think were key for them developing their particular fears. These will be significant relational events that have crystalised the frightened feelings they have about loving or being loved. For example, one man remembered missing his mother desperately, when at the age of five he was away from her for two months. However, when his mother met him at the train station she was in an angry mood and so didn't show delight in seeing him. This was a significant relational event from which the child formed a core belief that it is not safe to love, as the pain is awful when it is not reciprocated. As a result, he developed a fear of intimacy.

Where appropriate, participants could think about sharing their key memories with the person with whom they are in a personal relationship. Hopefully, this will enable the latter to be more compassionate towards them in the future. You may also like to talk to the participant about the natural flow of closeness to distance to closeness to distance that happens in relationships where people live together. To be more specific, there is a natural movement with periods of real intimacy, periods of separateness and periods of being together but not intimately. In a relationship where either party has fear of closeness or fear of distance, there can be a worry or even panic that the natural flow from one of these modes of being to the next will not happen. In other words, a person who has fear of emotional distance may become frightened that when they and their partner have to be apart, they may never reach intimacy again. So they may move into panic, criticism and blame when there is a long non-intimate period. The person frightened of intimacy may fear that they will somehow get stuck in being intimate and never move round to separateness again. As a result, they adopt a primitive flight mechanism.

Table 6.1 **Fear of intimacy**

Common core beliefs	Yes	Wants and needs	Yes
'If you let someone get close, they'll overwhelm you/control you/drain you/take from you in some way'		Long periods of time on my own	
Close relationships mean loss of freedom and feeling trapped		Space away from people	
To be safe in intimate relationships, you have be in control, not let them control you		Respect my need for separateness/withdrawal/alone time	
Getting close to someone means lots emotional demands. Closeness always carries obligations and pressures		To be allowed to go and know that friends/partners will still love me and welcome me when I return	
The more you give the more they'll want		For people to understand that after periods of closeness I may need to distance myself for a while. Please don't take this personally.	
Common fears		**Use of space and movement**	
Loss of self		The safety of a busy life/or geographical distance	
Feelings of powerlessness/helplessness		Being impossible to get hold of on the telephone, 'being unavailable'	
Engulfment/being taken over/overwhelmed		Spending a lot of time in the toilet	
No means of escape/nowhere to hide		Avoiding busy public spaces where I might experience a feeling of intrusion of personal space	
My expressions of affection, being taken as an invitation for the other person to move forward or intrude even more		Withdrawal which leads others to pursue	
Their insatiable demands will drain me/suck me dry. Feeling used		Finding reasons for 'I must be going' or for delayed return	
Behaviour which contributes to fears being realised (as it can provoke the other person to pursue/demand/criticise)		**Safety**	
Being secretive or withholding		Retreats into my own home/space/room/safe place	
Being cautious with shows of affection		Spaces without people	
Primitive modes of flight/ withdrawal		Wanting people to be there (to avoid my feeling lonely) as long as there are no demands for contact	
Reacting to requests as if they were demands		Attachment to things, rather than people: computer, books	
Frequently not being there, emotional absence or physical absence		Solitary hobbies e.g. fishing/the potting shed/playing music on my own	
Staying silent			
Common vocabulary/criticism		**Vital relational skills**	
'I need more space'		To know that if you let people get close, you can always negotiate for times apart and explain why it's so important to you (so they don't take it personally)	
'Tied down'		To find a way of saying no and staying rather than withdrawing or leaving	
'No room'		To state clearly what you feel	
'Trapped'		To be able to set boundaries/be confident in your capacity to say 'No'	
'Too demanding'		To be able to say 'What I need now is . . .'	
'Feeling suffocated'		To bring about negotiated withdrawals rather than sudden unexplained leavings	

Table 6.2 **Fear of emotional distance**

Common core beliefs	Yes	Wants and needs	Yes
People you love will always leave you in the end		To be taken care of	
I'm basically unlovable		To be pursued/sought after	
I try so hard to make someone want to be with me – please/control/always work on my appearance		To be loved unconditionally	
'If s/he leaves me, I'll never find anyone else as lovely'		To be seen as really special	
People will find me/ my needs too much		For times of blissful union to go on and on	
Common fears		**Use of movement and space**	
Rejection		Wanting togetherness not liking aloneness	
Love going cold		Seeking out/pursuing the loved person	
Aloneness		Rushing towards then rushing away, then rushing towards again	
Being unwanted/uninvited		Waiting for the loved person to seek me out/contact me	
Not mattering		Not trusting someone will come towards me/ring back/write back/return/stay etc . . .	
Never having an intimate relationship again		Resigned to being the one who always does the reaching out	
Dying alone			
Behaviour which contributes to fears being realised		**Safety**	
Rushing towards		Peopled spaces	
Frequently needing proofs of love		Someone you love telling you they love you	
Being demanding		Someone staying and not going	
Frequent complaints of not getting enough e.g. love/appreciation/affection/attention		Being in their arms	
Repeated need for reassurance		Being in their mind	
Common vocabulary/sentiment		**Vital self-support**	
'I need more from you'		To remember to stand still rather than rush towards	
'It's not enough'		To get on with changing your own life, rather than trying to change them	
'I want to spend more time together'		To wait, to give them the chance to reach out to you	
'Do you love me?'		To hold in mind that intense fear of emotional distance is fuelled by unmet needs in childhood.	
'What do you feel?'			

Fear of being in groups

■Objective

This exercise is for those people who want to explore why being in groups feels so painful for them, with a view, then, to having the courage to join groups in a less anxious way in the future, to find their voice in a current group or to be different in groups now to how they have been in groups in the past.

Participants who fear being in groups need to know that if you have had a bad experience of a group in the past, it is normal to feel anxiety about going into a group. (We fear in the future what actually happened in the past.)

For many people groups trigger (not always in conscious awareness) painful feelings of their very first group, namely their family. Sometimes exploring and identifying this is the first point in tackling the fear. It can also help to give the participant some key information about groups, as some fears are, of course, in part grounded in reality. The following will be of interest to some participants and can be useful if discussed in terms of any personal resonances:

The truth about groups?

- Groups will at times replicate negative family experiences.
- Groups can amplify aggressive feelings. Freud called it 'amplification of drives' (think of gangs).
- The bigger the group the less observing ego – so gang violence, football crowds, etc.
- The sensible thinking self can get lost and an amplification of primitive forces can prevail (think of *Lord of the Flies*, some of the terrible things groups do in war or of in situations of intolerance of difference).
- In groups more intense, sharply focused feelings common to early childhood can come to the fore – sibling rivalry, envious attacks, murderous rage, or feeling lost, alone and isolated.
- There is contagion in groups – anything negative spreads quickly.

- When groups, e.g. groups of bullies, use collective negative power against an individual, it's one of the worst psychological pains that individual can feel.

It is also useful for participants who fear groups to know that if we avoid groups altogether we avoid some of the most powerfully positive experiences possible.

The positive aspect of some groups

- When group members have sophisticated social skills, then profoundly moving help for and support of people can take place.
- When there is a synergy of creative energy with group members, incredible vision, creativity and drive can result in the most amazing products, services, organisations, acts of goodness, positive cultural shifts and social change.

■Instructions to give the participant

Too many of us have never had someone listen to us about our experiences of groups across a lifetime. Yet the groups we have been part of can be hugely influential in terms of our feelings about our self, others and life in general. So this exercise provides this key listening time.

Think of times you have been in a group in terms of how what happened in that group may be fuelling your fear and possible avoidance of groups today.

Look at the picture. Under the title 'Fear of being in groups', write a list of all the groups you have been a member of in the past. Use a colon followed by the feelings you had in that group. So, for example:

Girl Guides: Rejected
Class at school: Not accepted
Family: No voice

Then think of what your fears of being in groups are now and write these in the white circle entitled 'What is the fear/What might happen'. In case you are stuck, here are some common fears people have in groups.

Common fears about being in groups

I will get lost because of so many people here have so much to say/opinions/feelings/ideas.
I will lose myself, my identity, my self-worth in this group (too noticed/too seen/too unappreciated).
I will be rejected.
I will be scapegoated.
I will be humiliated/shamed.
I can control another person and then I feel safe, but I can't control a group.
I can't breathe in groups, like I am drowning in a sea of other people's needs.

Now look at what the common themes are between what actually happened in the groups you were a member of in the past and your residual fears about groups today.

How have you generalised from the specific meaning your mind tells you that because the bad thing happened in *that* group it will happen in all groups?
How have these past experiences contributed to your fear of groups now?
How could you dare to be different in the next group?
Do you ever act in groups in ways that actually invite a replay of your past?
Do you, for example, ever put yourself on the outside of the group (expecting rejection) when in fact the group wants to invite you to come in?

■Development – Further exploration of the influence of the first group (the family)

Many participants will appreciate you listening to them about how they were in their first group (their family), particularly if it resembles how they are in groups now.

When participants are fascinated by how they are replaying in groups today what happened in their first group, their family, you might help them with more exploration of this theme. Ask them to recall the emotional atmospheres in their family of mealtimes, family holidays, bedtimes, going to school, being met at school, doing homework. Ask them to tell you about these if they want to.

Fear of being in groups

What is the fear?
What might happen?

-
-
-
-
-
-

Figure 6.3

Fear of being myself in case I am too much

■Objective

The myth of excessive fragility is a fear-based belief that you cannot ever really be yourself, say what you really feel, because people are not emotionally strong enough to take it. If you were to get angry, for example, or assert your needs or opinions, the belief is that the other person would fall apart in some way or move into some kind of volcanic anger. This myth frequently originates from a childhood where a parent was so emotionally volatile that the child learnt to protect both the parent and themselves. The child usually does this by ensuring that they have only 'nice' feelings all the time. Hence, they develop what is known as 'a false self' (Winnicott, 1964). This often develops over time after the child has repeatedly witnessed the parent breaking down in some way (known as collapsive) or exploding (known as retaliate), when the child showed anything other than compliance and obedience. Often the whole family walks on eggshells around such a parent.

Sometimes the myth of excessive fragility is compounded by someone saying something like 'You'll make your mother ill' or 'You have made your Dad's depression worse by being so inconsiderate', or by an event which collides with the child's particular thought or deed. For example, a child is particularly naughty one day and the next day, quite coincidentally, mum gets the flu. The child then thinks he caused it. This is known as 'magical thinking'. Or the child has a secret thought about wanting his sibling dead, and quite coincidentally the sibling has an accident. From such events the child generalises from the specific: 'I am so powerful, and other people are so fragile'. Then throughout life, unless the 'myth of excessive fragility' is challenged, even emotionally robust people can be seen in this way. They too must be protected from the person's supposedly dangerous emotions. As a result, all healthy assertiveness,

natural protest, potency and difference of opinion must be squashed or stifled for fear of upsetting. In actuality the person who suffers from the myth of excessive fragility is frightened both of damaging but also of being damaged by the other person's reaction to them, which they fear to be some kind of emotional outburst or terrible collapse. The first step to giving up this myth is to become aware that you have it in the first place. This exercise supports that.

■Instructions to give the participant

Feeling that you can't be real with people in your life who matter, that you have to rein yourself in somehow and have smaller, politer emotions than the ones you are actually having, can be a real burden and block development of self and of those key relationships in your life. The first step to changing this often well-established pattern of relating (usually stemming from childhood) is to heighten awareness of what exactly you are doing in these relationships and why being the authentic you feels so dangerous.

Think of a person or people in your life, past and present, with whom you feel or have felt you cannot be yourself. You dare not be real with them. You dare not say what you feel, state what you need, or confront them appropriately.

Look at the picture. Think of people in your life with whom you feel you can't be real. On each line in the 'My fears' box, write down the name of a particular person you have brought to mind. Underneath each name in turn, write what you imagine might happen if you suddenly were real with this person – if you said what you really felt, expressed your hurt, anger, resentment, for example. Which seems to be your greater fear overall, that they will collapse (break down, cry) or that they will retaliate (explode in anger)? From the exercise consider how your childhood relationships may have contributed to you needing to protect people from you in this way.

Fear of being myself in case I am too much

Figure 6.4

Without a voice

■Objective

This exercise is for people who fear speaking in groups and/or can't voice what they really want to say in relationships, sometimes because they don't know what they feel, think or what their opinions are. The exercise can be particularly beneficial for people who believe that if they say what they feel and need, the other person will react very badly, turn away in some way, recoil or get angry. A useful literary reference that people can often relate to is in Charles Dickens's *Oliver Twist* when Oliver dares to find his voice and says, 'Please sir, I want some more' and the master explodes with rage.

When the fear is of speaking in groups

Usually what is happening here is that something from the childhood family is being replayed. Usually, original events in the family group led to feeling deeply shamed and so the person fears being shamed all over again in other groups. Common fears are that if I say something:

- I will be criticised for saying the wrong thing.
- I will get rejected.
- I'm not worth listening to.
- I'm not worth anyone's attention.
- If I am noticed I will be shamed. (The irony is that if you are silent in a group you are guaranteed to get noticed!)
- There is no point in my saying this because someone has already said it and they said it better than me (inferiority).

In fact, so many people were not listened to in childhood or told be quiet. So they didn't have a voice or they had it taken away from them because they were shut down. This may not just be parents; it can be siblings, bullies or teachers, too. Or sometimes a trauma in the original family or later on in school life was so awful that the child is rendered speechless because whatever happened felt too overwhelming and no one helped them process and make sense of what happened. There is a neuroscientific basis to this. In trauma, systems close down and the Broca's area in the brain (speech centre) shuts down so that we are literally speechless.

People who have been brought up to not have their own opinions and feelings separate from those of other may find this exercise difficult. They may be out of touch with what their own needs, thoughts, feelings and opinions are! They may only know what other people want them to want, feel and think! However, thinking about these things now in this way can be a vital first step to acknowledging them and then to developing the capacity for both authenticity and assertiveness.

■Instructions

In the 'Worst phantasies' circle write what your worst fears and phantasies are if you did speak out, voice opinions, thoughts and feelings in a group or in an important relationship, e.g. no one would listen to you or laugh at you or reject you.

In light of this, what outdated beliefs about yourself or other people do you need to challenge? What events in your past and in particular your childhood are fuelling your fears and phantasies today?

Now think of times in the past when you would have dearly loved to say something and didn't. Write what those things are in the second circle. Now think of current situations and relationships in your life, what would you like to say and to whom (things you are not saying at the moment because of your fears). What support and help do you need to actually say them?

■Development – Finding your 'voice' game

So often people who feel they have no voice feel defeated and demoralised. They have lost touch with (or never had in the first place) their natural assertiveness.

In light of this, a strong speaking-out game is often useful. This must be an embodied response; hence, a suitable development for some participants will be the Yes/No game. The rules are as follows: You say 'yes' in a very quiet voice and ask the participant to say 'no' in a louder voice than you. You then say your 'yes' a bit louder than their 'no'. You encourage them to say 'no' louder than your 'yes', and so on, until the participant is very confidently and strongly saying 'no', hopefully in a very believable way. When this works, the participant will then be able to feel what assertiveness is from their gut and connect to their own potency in this way. You can follow this on by getting the participant to say to you, 'I will not put up with this!'

A thin voice that carries little conviction often means a participant has cut off from their body due to chronic fear at some time in their life. Even after you have given the participant some voice coaching, if you find that their voice still has no natural authority, then change tack. Move to an exercise such as 'Toxic shame' (let them choose one that resonates with them) to explore the childhood influences that have squashed or discouraged their natural assertiveness. They may need to work through their feelings of shame and fear, grieving for their child self, before they are able to find their voice.

Figure 6.5

Mistrust

■Objective

The objective of this exercise is to support people who block emotional connection with caring others due to mistrust. Most of us will trust doctors and surgeons with our bodies, pilots not to crash the planes we ride in, school staff not to harm our children, but some of us cannot trust enough in close relationships in case someone breaks our hearts.

People who live with mistrust keep emotional distance in relationships due to fear of being hurt, let down or betrayed just as has happened in their past. But their very defensiveness so often keeps out all the beautiful aspects of close relationship: feeling cherished, feeling deeply known and loved just for who you are. Moreover, it is hard to have a relationship with someone who doesn't trust, e.g. 'I am being open and engaging with you, but you are being closed and defended with me, so eventually I give up and go away'. Or as one woman said, 'I can have sex but I don't want to fall in love because it's too dangerous. So once I start having feelings, I end the relationship.'

To establish an emotional connection with someone the following has to take place:

I say personal things about me.
You say personal things about you.
I ask you questions about your life.
You ask me questions about my life.
I show curiosity/empathy in what you have said.
You show curiosity/empathy in what I have said.

If a person is mistrustful they are very unlikely to do the above, because saying personal things would make them too vulnerable, too open to the possibility of negative reactions. So there can be no real emotional connection, and so no feeding of the soul in vital ways. The result is loneliness.

The first step to moving from mistrust to trust is to be aware of the underlying fear and memories fuelling the mistrust. This exercise supports this awareness.

■Instructions

Trust and getting close to someone is a huge issue for some people. This is particularly the case when too many people have let them down in some way, rejected them, abandoned or betrayed them or been too demanding, controlling or intrusive.

But living with mistrust, fuelled by pain from the past, can have a high price. It can block real emotional connection and leave us only with communications at a banal, polite level of bland, safe feelings. Then we miss out on the beautiful aspects of close relationships – feeling cherished, feeling deeply known, loved just for who you are – and we live instead with loneliness.

In order to shift from a fixed position of mistrust to trust, the first step is to consider what is fuelling your mistrust. For many people the mistrust started with parents. For others it happened later in life with partners or friends. In either case they dared to love and then got very hurt. It's never too late to move on to daring to trust, but it can be hard to get there without addressing what from the past is fuelling your fears.

So, in the picture, write in the white circle behind one of the figure's backs, all the fears you have about close emotional connection, about being vulnerable and open and deepening your relationship with people you like or have really liked, turning towards them fully, so to speak. In case it's hard to think, here are some things other people wrote in the white circle:

- Fear of being hurt, rejected, used, treated as an' it'
- Fear of being shamed, humiliated, made fun of
- Fear of being betrayed

- Fear of being 'left again'
- Being told as a child 'Men only want one thing – sex. Never trust men'

If you like, talk about how you might now move on from this emotional baggage and dare to love/connect again. How can you dare, but this time establish some level of psychological safety, e. g. support figures, albeit knowing that there are no guarantees in love and friendship?

■Development – Psycho-education and discussion points for issues of mistrust

A very useful exercise in this chapter, which can be explored alongside this one, is 'Fear of closeness and fear of distance'.

Discussion points

Talk about the inherent messy and unpredictable nature of close relationships but 'better to have loved and lost than never loved at all', or the Irish proverb, 'When mistrust comes in love goes out'.

If mistrust feels chronic and fixed, talk about the particular benefits of counselling or therapy to address this. Sometimes the only way to shift deep-seated mistrust is to be in the safest relationship context there is, namely counselling or therapy. Here you can begin to trust through experiencing repeated empathic responses over time. This will usually be experienced as the power of contrast, between the very psychologically safe person now and the people who felt so very unsafe in your past. Through good therapy or counselling you can begin to understand that relating to people can be a source of deep contentment rather than fear. Good therapy or counselling will provide many opportunities to practise a whole range of different forms of emotional connection, both more playful forms and deeper ways of knowing someone truly understands your pain and finds the words to say it. I will give the last word to the famous child clinician, Dan Hughes, whose work covers

in-depth support for very troubled children to move from blocked trust to trust. He speaks from the child here:

> Wow. Something weird is going on here when I interact with this [adult] that is so different from the way things went with [other adults] so maybe, just maybe it would be all right to trust these guys and stop being so mistrusting.

> (Baylin and Hughes, 2016: 45)

Mistrust

Figure 6.6

Further reading

Baylin, J. and Hughes, D. (2016) *The Neurobiology of Attachment-Focused Therapy: Enhancing connection & trust in the treatment of children & adolescents.* New York: W. W. Norton & Co.

Tools and techniques to improve and repair relationships

■About the resources in this chapter

Intimacy, like everything else, requires art.

(Moore, 1994a)

In order to enjoy long-term, satisfying relationships in which both parties develop emotionally and socially over time, you need some key skills and resources. This is the case with all forms of significant relationships, whether it is parent and child, sibling and sibling, friend and friend or intimate adult relationship.

Some of the exercises in this chapter are designed for two participants to work together on their relationship, to improve and/or repair. These exercises may, for example, be useful for parent and child, two work colleagues or a couple to do together. The relationship skills are practised initially with the guidance of the practitioner. It is then hoped that these skills will become a potent resource for the two people to do on their own in their ongoing relationship.

The art of relationship (for one person)

■Objective

This exercise aims to help the participant to consider the relationship skills that they bring to important relationships in their life. It is designed to support the participant to celebrate their strengths and to consider their weaknesses in terms of what would be good to add to their 'relationship skills resources'. The exercise will also be useful for people who repeatedly find themselves in unsatisfying, painful or destructive relationships, or who keep choosing people who are unable to sustain or develop a close relationship.

■Instructions to give the participant

Fill in 'The art of relationship' table. Tick the relational skills that you think you do have and are able to use well in your relationships. Find a way of praising yourself for these, as it is easy to take them for granted. Then look at the skills and abilities that you find difficult. It can then be useful to talk about the reasons why this is the case. Did you have poor modelling of these particular relational skills in childhood and/or later in life? If so, think of someone in your life now who would be a good role model for the skills and abilities you want to develop. Finally, if you are considering the emotional health of an important relationship in your life now, you may also like to fill in the table in terms of what you perceive to be that person's relational skills and abilities.

The art of relationship

This table is based on Jaak Panksepp's positive arousal systems in the limbic part of the brain, namely CARE, SEEKING and PLAY. When these systems are optimally activated we can experience the most sublime range of feelings due to the neurochemical base of these systems, namely opioids, oxytocin and dopamine. When working together these neurochemicals give us a sense of 'all is well in our world' and an energised engagement in life. So if we are able to 'go there' with another person, or take them there, our relationship will be rich indeed. The table also includes a section on 'relational repair' and key conversational skills that are also key to sustain strong emotional connection with someone over time.

Table 7.1 **The art of relationship**

Tick 'yes' to the statements that depict a relationship skill of yours. Tick 'No' if you feel you a particular relationship skill is difficult or not within your range at the moment.	Yes	No
CARE (nurturing)		
Ability to empathise and express genuine warmth over time		
Ability to listen well, imagine things from the other person's point of view, how they see events		
Ability to comfort, soothe and express concern when the other person is upset		
SEEKING (explorative drive)		
Ability to make things happen for both of you, outings, new experiences, surprises		
'Let's!' A sense of exploration and shared energised engagement in the world		

Table 7.1 (Continued)

TOOLS AND TECHNIQUES

Tick 'yes' to the statements that depict a relationship skill of yours. Tick 'No' if you feel you a particular relationship skill is difficult or not within your range at the moment.	Yes	No
PLAY (and playing with ideas)		
Ability to be playful and spontaneous		
Ability to engage in high intensity positive arousal states		
Shared joy, excitement and enthusiasm		
Ability for humour/shared laughter		
ABILITY TO REPAIR THINGS AFTER CONFLICT		
Ability to express anger, hurt or irritation in a clear non-blaming way focusing on resolution and ways forward e.g. 'When you, I feel . . .		
Ability to own your part in things, knowing that painful situations in close relationships are very often co-created		
Ability to 'truth listen'* and hear feedback without getting defensive		
Ability to negotiate and compromise when there's a clash of needs		
Ability to mend attachment ruptures/misattunements and apologise for hurt caused		
CONVERSATIONAL SKILLS		
I say personal things about me		
(You say personal things about you)		
When you say personal things about you I respond with interest and appropriate empathy		
I ask you questions about your life (curiosity)		
(You ask me questions about my life)		
When you answer my questions about your life, I listen with interest and use words to acknowledge I have listened and hopefully understood		
I acknowledge, empathise and show curiosity in what you say		
(You acknowledge, empathise and show curiosity in what I say)		

* Definition of truth listening (rather than being a lie invitee): The couple therapist Ellyn Bader (2001) gives a very clear example of the ability to 'truth listen'. The couple in question were struggling in their relationship because of a buildup of unspoken resentments. The wife dared to say, 'I have been praying for your death'. The husband could have come back with all manner of sarcasm: 'Well thanks a lot'; or attacks: 'You vicious cow', 'You are just full of bile'. But he just listened, reflected, and then said in a quiet voice, 'How long have you been praying?'

At that moment, the woman knew the relationship was workable. What a relational skill indeed, when someone can listen so well to painful feedback with such openness, resisting the pull to lash back or move into a cold withdrawal to defend against the hurt they feel.

■Other models of relational health and ability for emotional connection

Professor John Gottman (University of Washington) carried out over 40 years of scientific-based research on predicting divorce, looking at the key components of marital stability and on how to build emotional connection with another person over time. The participant may be interested in Gottman's work, again in light of their own skills or lack of them and how they might want to 'skill up'. So you might like to discuss these with the participant. Gottman's research showed that two people who deepen and develop emotional connection over time (he refers to them as masters at relationship) had the following relational skills:

1 *Curiosity in terms of what matters to the other person about their life, their relationships, their hopes and dreams, etc.* For example: 'How do you feel about your job/being a father' rather than 'Can you pick the kids up tonight?'
2 *Voiced admiration/respect/affection and gratitude* for the little things as well as the big things (instead of taking them for granted). For example: 'Thank you for doing the washing up'.
3 *Turning towards:* This is a lovely and subtle notion of being able to respond well when your partner turns towards you for emotional connection. Gottman calls it making 'emotional bids'. These can range from a seemingly small bid of 'Oh look at that beautiful flower' to 'Can you help me with this really big problem I have at work'. He found that if partners turn away (grunt, say nothing) when their partner turns towards them, they don't re-bid. It's too painful.

If both people in a relationship are skilled at the above, Gottman has found in his research that these become protective factors when there are conflicts and misattunments in the relationship. For more on this, see John Gottman's 'Making marriage work', which is available as a video: www.youtube.com/watch?v=AKTy PgwfPgg&t=37s.

Further reading

Gottman, J. (2018) *The Seven Principles for Making Marriage Work: A practical guide*. London: Orion Spring.

The 'when you . . . I feel' exercise (for two people)

■ Objective

This exercise aims to help two people to establish far better contact with each other. Some may find it useful for interactive repair after a period of painful, hurtful and angry feelings that have never been resolved. Others may find it valuable in addressing issues that have never been fully talked about.

The structure of the exercise means that both parties can express feelings safely, albeit strongly, if they so wish. The structure also keeps the two people focused on resolution, not blame. In blaming ('How could you be so heartless, when I'm feeling so low?') people rarely state clearly what they want, so they don't get what they want! In contrast, in this task both people state their needs clearly and specifically.

■ Instructions to give the participant

What to say to the two people:

Think of things in your relationship that you want to change, things that you find difficult about the other person and things that you may not have said before because it felt too unsafe to do so. This exercise will give you a safe structure to say some of these things. As I am here with the two of you, I will also be part of that safe structure.

Number yourselves 1 and 2. Number 1 will start by finishing the sentences below. You cannot say anything else. You have to keep very strictly to the four sentences. Number 2 just listens.

- When you . . .
- I feel . . .
- So what I want is . . .
- Will you . . .?

Example

- When you always leave me to clear out the cat's litter tray
- I feel treated as a servant
- So what I want is for us to take turns doing it
- Will you do that?

Number 2 then answers the question 'Will you . . .?' The two people discuss the answer. Then number 2 takes their turn. Continue alternating, following the energy of the couple, until they feel that for the moment they have addressed enough of their issues.

Important technical points

1 Both parties can only speak within this set format. This prevents them spiralling into yet more anger, hurt and miscommunication as in the common attacks of 'You are this/you are that', 'It's all your fault' and 'If it weren't for you . . . '.
2 With the 'So what I want' sentence, the temptation is just to say something unhelpfully general like 'I just want you to love me more'. Statements such as this are likely to be disguised blame. If you generalise, e.g. 'I want you to be more loving', it also does not give the other person enough information as to the exact nature of your request/need: what loving would look like for you, how you want the love expressed, and how often. So the couple may need some guidance on this point.
3 With the 'Will you?' question, if the answer is 'No I won't', the person will need to explain why not. They can be encouraged to give or compromise in another area of the relationship. Or they can say, 'I will think

about it' and give the other person a time when they will get an answer. Or they may say 'I am happy to do *x* but with the following conditions'. In short, you are empowering the two people to find healthier options in dealing with difficulties and conflicts and to develop more skills in negotiation for future conflicts that will inevitably arise between them.

The 'unfinished sentence' exercise (for two people)

■Objective

This exercise is designed to ease communication and to facilitate a deeper and more authentic level of connection between two people in an established relationship. If a parent is doing the exercise with their child, give the child the option of drawing their answers rather than speaking them. If the child chooses this option, he or she may prefer the parent to follow suit.

■Instructions to give to the participants

I'll give you both some unfinished sentences. I will ask A to finish the sentences first. You can say your answer, or do a super-quick drawing for your answer, or a combination of both. If you don't want to finish one of the sentences you can just say 'pass'. B should just listen to what A says without speaking. At the end of the list I will give B some unfinished sentences to help B to respond to what A has said. Then we will begin again, this time with B finishing the sentences.

Here are A's sentences:

- I like it when you . . .
- I don't like it when you . . .
- I love it when you . . .
- I like it when together we . . .
- I wish together we could . . .
- I want you to know that . . .
- I wish you knew that . . .

- It feels like you don't understand that . . .
- I am frightened of you when you . . . (Don't give this sentence to a parent to answer if you are working with parent and child, as it can burden and worry the child.)
- I feel angry with you when . . .
- I feel good when you . . .
- I feel like rubbish when you . . .
- I feel sad when you . . .
- I feel sad that we never seem to do . . . anymore.
- If I had three wishes for you they would be . . .
- If I had three wishes for me they would be . . .
- If I had three wishes for us they would be . . .
- One of my best times with you was . . . (good to finish on a positive note)

Okay, it's B's chance to respond. B, having listened to A, can you finish these sentences in response to what A has said? You will not be able to move out of the sentence stems.

- I was surprised when you said . . .
- I didn't know that you felt . . .
- I was sorry to hear that . . .
- I feel hurt that . . .
- Thank you for letting me know that . . .
- I am delighted to hear that you . . .
- I agree with you when you said that . . .
- I am really thinking about what you said about . . .

If you are working with a parent and child, only do this exercise if you know the parent will be appropriate in their answers, provide the child with a good relational experience overall, and not burden the child with their own worries, anxieties or a barrage of unspoken resentments, anger, lectures on behaviour, etc. You may speak to the parent before the session, to ensure they know what is expected of them, and to establish the necessary boundaries.

The following additional aspect can be particularly helpful if you are working with children who are coping with a parent's raw feelings of depression, fear or anger, which are spilling out in the family home. But only do this if you feel the parent can hear what the child is saying without feeling threatened and lashing out in self-protective anger. Ask the child to do a 'super-quick drawing answer' for each of these unfinished sentences (unless of course they prefer just to speak their answers, but this can be far scarier).

Daddy/Mummy:

- When you get sad I feel . . .
- When you get angry I feel . . .
- When you get scared I feel . . .
- I enjoy . . .
- I feel worried when . . .
- I feel angry when . . .
- I love it when together we . . .

The parent needs to listen to the whole list of sentences. In their response, ask them to use the safe structure of the unfinished sentences in B's 'chance to respond' section in the main exercise. Don't reverse this by asking the parent to finish the sentences. This is because the child could feel further burdened by parental feelings.

As practitioner, it will be important for you to comment on the 'big feelings' in the session after both people have finished the exercise, being most careful not to take sides. It may also be appropriate after you have done this to ask both people if you have failed to comment on something that was very important to either of them. It is also good to ask them before the end of the session if they want to say anything to each other, draw anything for each other or do anything with each other as a way of finishing. People often do amazing things at the eleventh hour. But don't ask this question if doing so would open up more pain which there isn't time to work through. Keep using the unfinished sentence structure right to the end of the session if you feel the two people need a structure to keep them interacting with each other positively, not negatively.

The 'like / don't like it' game (for two people)

■ Objective

This exercise offers a wonderful safety net for the working through of painful, hurt or angry feelings, provided that there is a basis of goodwill in the relationship. (If not, don't choose this exercise.) The exercise is particularly useful if one or both people fear angry exchanges.

After completing the exercise people invariably remark how supportive this structure has been for them and how they have felt really heard by the other person. (People so often do not escalate into self-protective anger, if they feel heard.)

■ Instructions to give the participant

Each person agrees to listen to the other in turn without interrupting.

1 Person A holds the watch and times three minutes. They are asked to keep the time, say when to start and when the three minutes are up. Their role is also to listen carefully to what the other person says, in silence, without interrupting or speaking.

2 When the three minutes start, person B expresses their resentments to person A, starting every sentence with one of the following: 'I don't like it when you . . . '; 'I feel angry when you . . . '; I feel hurt when you . . . '. This prevents B getting into destructive put-downs of sentences that start with 'You are . . . ' (e.g. 'You are a selfish/stupid . . . etc.').

3 At the end of the first three minutes, person A says 'Stop'. Then person B moves into the second three minutes, starting every sentence with 'I like it when you . . . '; 'I value when you . . . '; 'I love it when you . . . '. Then they voice all their appreciations about person A. Person A then announces when the three minutes are up.

4 A and B swap roles – so B keeps the time whilst A shares personal resentments for three minutes and then appreciations for another three minutes.

Before starting, tell the two people that it is fine if there are periods of silence when either party is speaking. The three-minute structure is still maintained.

Because of the appreciations placed at the end of the exercise, both parties are usually left in a contemplative rather than angry mood. Each then has a further three minutes to comment on what has been said. (If you think either party is going to go into attack and blame, use the structure of the 'chance to respond' sentences that are listed in the exercise called 'The unfinished sentence' exercise.)

This exercise is often a very moving experience. Appreciations can be bottled up just as much as resentments. When eventually expressed, they can move the person who expresses them just as much as the listener.

■ More about the 'I appreciate' part of the exercise

One key role in working with two people together, whether parent and child or adult partner and adult partner or other relationship, is to support both parties to express stored-up, unspoken positive feelings about the other, not just negative. When this happens, both the giver and the receiver are often moved to tears. As one teenage daughter said to her mother, 'I didn't realise I was sitting on such a lot of thank-yous!' Both parties often realise how much poorer they would have been without such a sharing, and how it is as easy to bottle up positive feelings as it is negative ones. Yet for some people, feelings of love or gratitude can carry a tension, fear and dread because of the sheer strength of the feeling. As one grateful husband put it, 'My gratitude to my wife is so huge, it's as if, metaphorically speaking, I don't have enough vases for all the flowers she brings me'. It is indeed a courageous and risky business to express such feelings, as a generous reception can never be guaranteed. As a mother said, 'I had to go into counselling when I realised I couldn't tell my son that I loved him. I was terrified he might despise me for it, just like my father had.'

The empathy game (for two people)

■Objective

If negative feelings in a close relationship remain unresolved, if the atmosphere is full of unexpressed emotion, or if it feels too scary to share anger and resentments, then the empathy game can be a real help. In this exercise, each person tries to empathise with what the other person might be feeling. Feeling understood can have a remarkable effect on melting hardened and bitter feelings. However, be sure that both people have a basic capacity for empathy and concern before choosing this exercise. Without this, the exercise could drive the two people farther apart, not move them closer together.

The exercise is not suitable for parent and child, as empathy is in part a frontal lobe executive function, which only develops in children as they get older. It can, however, be used effectively with self-aware, emotionally literate teenagers and their parents.

■Instructions to give the participant

Person A has three minutes to voice their empathy in terms of what they imagine person B might be feeling about a painful issue in the relationship. After three minutes, switch roles, so Tony (person B) imagines what Mary (person A) is feeling. They then share with each other the aspects of the empathy that were right and amazingly right and wrong, and wrong.

Example

Mary: I can imagine Tony that you may be feeling really angry because I promised to take the kids out today, but then I had to do something for work. I never thanked you for dealing so well with the change of plans at the last minute. And I can imagine you may be feeling very frustrated with me because I keep forgetting to get the holiday brochures as I promised. Perhaps you are feeling de-prioritised in some way, feeling that I don't really want to go on holiday with you, but I do. I really do.

Tony then gives feedback on what has been said, in terms of accuracy and inaccuracy and of how much he feels understood/misunderstood.

Tony: I was amazed that you got it exactly right about the holiday brochure. Thank you for understanding. The bit about the kids was nearly right, but the feeling you missed was . . .

People often report feeling amazed at the accuracy of the other person's empathy and how soothed they feel by the understanding. Many problems in relationships stem from not feeling understood, not getting through or not feeling heard.

Our best and worst times (for two people)

■ Objective

This exercise is for two people and is also suitable for parent and child, regardless of age. It is often a real help for two people to stand back and think about their positive and negative ways of relating. It also offers an opportunity for both people to reflect on what is working well in their relationship and what is not working well. By considering things in this way it is hoped that the two people can put more energy into the shared activities and ways of relating that are good for them and avoid the things that may be harming their relationship.

■ Instructions to give the participant

Give each person a very large piece of paper (A1 size is ideal). Tell them that they will be working on their own for the first part of the exercise. Ask them each to draw a line down the middle of their piece of paper. On the left side of the paper write, 'Best times with you' and on the right, 'Worst times with you'. Give them just ten minutes (time structure adds to the safety of the exercise) to do drawings or write words for both sides of the picture. When they have finished, ask each person in turn to talk about/show what they have written or drawn. The other person must remain silent to ensure the highest quality listening. After this, both can ask any questions they like, so that they are clear about what the other person has done. The two people can then discuss what they have drawn and what the other person has drawn. Ask them to comment on what surprised

them, hurt them, moved them, pleased them, etc. Here are some questions you might ask:

- Having looked at both your sets of images, what have you learned about your relationship? What are the similarities and the differences in terms of what you have drawn/written?
- Is there something that the other person has done in their image that surprised you or doesn't surprise you?
- Is there anything you would like to change in your relationship, do more of or do less of as a result of what you have done here?

Then ask both people how they could share more best times and what they can do to prevent a repetition of worst times.

Example

Here is an example of nine-year-old Billy's best and worst times with his mum:

Billy: *Best times with you* – playing, shopping, just you and me; listening when I am sad; making a cake together; when we laugh about something; when we go to the coffee shop in the park and talk about stuff; when you tickle me.

Billy: *Worst times with you* – when you are sad; when you are with my brother and not me; when you are on the phone all the time; when you do the cleaning, not playing; when you nag me to do my homework.

As a result of this, the practitioner supported Billy in asking his mum for an hour's quality time each evening. She was very moved and agreed that she needed to do more playing and give up some of her obsession with cleaning.

■Development – Communicating through colour cards

When working with a parent and child it can be useful to support a child who is not able to speak about his feelings well with a different system of communication. Show the child how he can use colour cards. For example, instead of moving into challenging behaviour when he needs attention, he just slips a red card into his mum's hand. When he hands her a yellow card it means 'I am hurt', a blue card means 'Can we talk?', a purple card means 'I need help not to blow with my anger'. It's great to help the child make the cards himself and draw things on them, so that he and his mum/dad remember what each card means.

Theories of motivation (for two people)

■Objective

A vital part of any emotionally healthy relationship is for both people to know that at times they will have very different experiences of the same event. They will also inevitably have some paranoid theories (fuelled by painful past experiences) about the other person's actions and intentions. These are known as 'theories of motivation based on emotional impact' (Resnick, 1998). This means we read certain intentions into the actions of the other person based on what these actions make us feel, the emotional impact they have on us. The problem in 'reading' the other person's intentions in this way is that we can often be totally inaccurate. This can cause all sorts of unnecessary pain and hurt. To prevent this, two people in a close relationship need to perfect the art of checking up their theories of motivation. Here are some examples of theories of motivation from actual couples, which were all highly inaccurate:

- 'I felt annoyed by him [emotional impact], therefore he wanted to annoy me.' [theory of motivation]
- 'I felt hurt by him [emotional impact], therefore he meant to hurt me.' [theory of motivation]
- 'When she didn't say goodbye properly, I felt insignificant to her [emotional impact]. I guess I don't mean very much to her.' [theory of motivation]

Such inaccurate theories of motivation informed by emotional impact are often fuelled by unworked-through painful childhood experiences, or later life trauma. Here is an example:

Tom: Mary, when you read your newspaper after our conversation, I felt totally rejected [emotional impact]. I hate how you reject me [theory of motivation], so that's why I stormed out and slammed the door.

Tom had often felt himself to be uninteresting to his parents in childhood. (They didn't know how to relate to children.) So when his wife read the newspaper, he immediately moved into believing that she actively wanted to reject him. Therefore, his theory about his wife's feelings was based purely on the impact her behaviour had on him. He then reacted to his 'theory of motivation' as if it was reality. He did not check his theory with her by asking her what she was actually feeling. He believed he had the absolute truth!

Unchecked theories of motivation are often the trigger for some of the most painful rows and misconnections in close relationships. For example, the man who has a theory of motivation that his partner is meaning to get rid of him may go and have an affair. If he had just checked his theory, he could have saved all three people terrible heartache and pain. In actuality, it was the 'truth' of his past that was colouring how he perceived the present.

■Instruction to the two participants

Decide who is going to go first. Okay, *x* is going first. So, think of a time recently when you had a thought or belief about what your partner [or whoever] feels about you. Tell the other person your belief and then check it out with them to see if you were right. Use this structure and finish these sentences:

- When you . . .
- I felt . . . [emotional impact]
- So my belief of what you feel/were feeling about me is . . . [theory of motivation]
- Am I right?

The other person then says whether they are right or wrong. If wrong, they are encouraged to say what they do feel. If there is a grain of truth in the other person's belief/theory of motivation, they should share this, and then it needs to be worked through compassionately. Ask the first person: 'What do you feel now, having checked out your belief? What do you feel having heard the other person's answer?' Then switch and the other person checks out their beliefs. Here is an example between a parent and child:

Billy (age eight): When you played with Nathan not me yesterday and you gave him a cuddle and not me, I felt horrid in my tummy. So I think that you must love him much more than me. Am I right?

Mum: You are wrong. In fact I was watching you with your Warhammer yesterday and I watched how carefully you were painting it, and I was thinking, wow what a super lovely kid Billy is. I am really sorry now that I didn't tell you that.

Practitioner: Billy, what do you feel now, having checked out what you imagined with Mum?

Billy doesn't say anything. He is too busy giving his mum a great big cuddle. So the message to the two people is, as soon as you feel a theory coming on, check it out, and then equally important, listen to the answer!

When the past spoils the present

If a person has a history of loss, trauma, separation, feeling unloved or relationships of emotional coldness, they may be particularly vulnerable to irrational theories of motivation that are not grounded in reality. So where one or both participants have this sort of history, it can be very useful to get them to speak about how the other person's actions have triggered an emotional pain from their past. This should only be done, however, where there is a strong basis of compassion and concern in the relationship.

Example

June: Derek, when you left without kissing me this morning, I worried you were going off me. Can I check that out?

Derek: You are completely wrong. I'm sorry, I was just really anxious about that meeting I had at work. [Gives June a hug.]

June: [The hug feels really warm and loving and makes her realise that her theory was wrong.]

Ask June whether she thinks an old childhood pain has been triggered by Derek's behaviour. June thinks it has. She explains to Derek that when she was a little girl, her father often left the house without saying goodbye to her and never sought her out to say hello when he came in at night. Hence, these painful images from her past were skewing her perception of her husband's behaviour. By June's self-revelation, Derek can understand much more about June's Achilles heel and so be more aware of and compassionate about her insecurities in this area.

Paper conversations

■Objective

This exercise is for two people to do together and is also suitable for parent and child. Because it engages the wisdom of the right brain, it often gets right to the heart of key issues in a relationship. It helps the two people to look closely at their habitual patterns of relating and to build an understanding of each other's relational needs. It is also a very useful exercise to help both people to see how fears and pain from the past may be adversely affecting their relationships.

■Instructions to give the participant

Ask the two people to sit opposite each other. Place a large piece of paper (A2 is the ideal size) on the table or floor between them. Also provide them with a box of crayons/felt-tip pens and some different colours of play dough. Then say to the two people: 'On this large piece of paper you will be having a special kind of conversation. The rules are as follows: Each of you picks a coloured pen and pot of play dough. Make sure you have chosen different colours from each other. All communication with each other will be done with the pens and play dough, no words! You can each alternate between pens and play dough as you choose. You might like to use just play dough or just pens or vary it. Please remain silent throughout. Decide who will start. The person who starts makes a mark on the paper using the pen or a piece of their play dough. The other person then replies, again using play dough or pens. The first person then replies to that statement and so on. The only rule is that there should be no marking the paper at the same time.'

As practitioner, watch what happens. There will be a lot going on very quickly, so you may just want to write down or draw the major relational events in your notes. These are the ones that seem to be the most emo-

tionally charged. You'll know which these are if you watch their body language, e.g. the participants giggle, grunt, look at each other, use force in the making of their marks. After a period of time, say ten minutes, stop the exercise. Then ask the two people to talk through what happened, starting at the beginning.

Typical practitioner statements to support the talking through include: 'Who went first? Is that typical in your relationship? What happened next? What did you feel when she moved away from you on the paper?' Then help the participants to check out their theories of motivation (see the 'Theories of motivation' exercise in this chapter).

Example

Pam and Peter are having some difficulties in their relationships. Peter was sent away to a boarding school when he was eight years old. He has been convinced all his life that it is because his mum didn't love him.

- Move 1. Peter does a big circle in the middle of the page.
- Move 2. Pam then does a jagged line nearby.
- Move 3. Peter then does a wiggly line close to Pam's.
- Move 4. Pam moves to the corner of the paper and draws some flowers.

There are many more moves but this gives you an example of how to proceed when a move evokes an emotional reaction from one or both parties.

Peter: [commenting on Pam's move 4] I thought Pam was fed up with me copying her, or that I was crowding her by being so close, so that is why she moved away and did those flowers.
Practitioner: Peter will you check that up with her? [checking up theory of motivation which has been based on impact]

Paper conversation

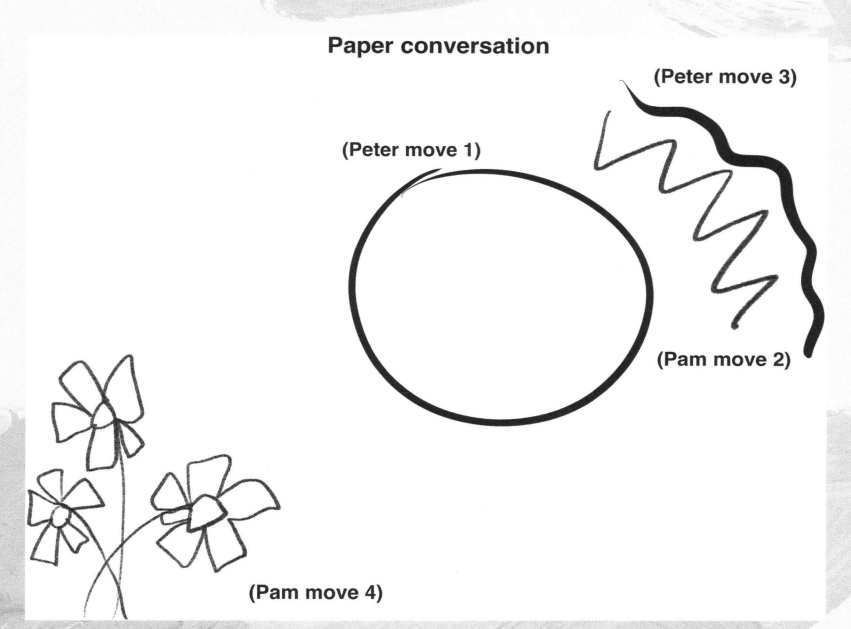

(Peter move 1)

(Peter move 3)

(Pam move 2)

(Pam move 4)

Figure 7.1

■Common relational issues

Peter: Pam, were you fed up of me? Is that why you moved so far away from me?

Pam: No, not at all, I thought you would find me intrusive if I continued to draw next to your drawing so that is why I did those little flowers at the other side of the paper.

Practitioner: How does it feel Peter to hear Pam say that?

Peter: Amazing. I was convinced her moving away was because I was crowding her!

Both parties are encouraged to keep checking up their beliefs as to why the other person acted as they did in the paper conversation. Sometimes someone's feelings may be proved right: 'Yes, I did move away because I found you clingy and invasive'. When this happens, continue as before: 'How do you feel, hearing that your fear about being clingy was true?' But then help them to reflect further: 'Does this ring any bells for you? Has this happened in other relationships?' If it is appropriate for you to work with childhood issues, you can ask, 'Do you know what childhood events are fuelling your need to cling in adult relationships?'

The practitioner can also ask if the feelings of being intruded on in the other person (let's say person B) are common and, if so, may once again be pain from past relationships being played out in the present. If person B has awareness about this, it could really help person A not to take person B's rejections so personally, and to be more compassionate about their need for emotional space.

Practitioner: Does that ring bells for you?

Person B: Oh yes. I have always had this thing about intrusion. My sister was so intrusive, always invading my privacy in some way.

Person A: Ah. Thanks for saying that. It helps me understand more now. It will help me to take it less personally from now on when you move away from me.

Bibliography

Allen, W. (Director) (1977) [film] *Annie Hall*.

Anda, R.,Williamson, D.,Jones, D.,Macera, C.,Eaker, E.,Glassman, A. andMarks, J. (1993) Depressed affect, hopelessness, and the risk of ischemic heart disease in a cohort of U.S. adults. Epidemiology,July, 4(4): 285–294.

Armstrong-Perlman, E. M. (1991) The allure of the bad object. *Free Associations* 2(3): 23.

Armstrong-Perlman, E. M. (1995) Psychosis: The sacrifice that fails? in Ellwood, J. (ed.) *Psychosis: Understanding and treatment*. London: Jessica Kingsley Publishers.

Aziz-Zadeh, L., Liew, S.-L. and Dandekar, F. (2012) Exploring the neural correlates of visual creativity. *Social Cognitive and Affective Neuroscience* 8: 475–480.

Bader, E. (2001) *Tell Me No Lies*. New York: Macmillan.

Bader M., Pearson P. and Schwartz J. (2001) *Tell Me No Lies: How to stop lying to your partner – and yourself – in the 4 stages of marriage*. New York: Sunlight Press.

Bar-Levav, R. (1990) *Thinking in the Shadow of Feelings*. London: Harper Collins.

Baylin, J. and Hughes, D. (2016) *The Neurobiology of Attachment-Focused Therapy: Enhancing connection & trust in the treatment of children & adolescents*. New York: W. W. Norton & Co.

Beckes, L., Ijzerman, H. and Tops, M. (2015) Toward a radically embodied neuroscience of attachment and relationships. *Front. Hum. Neurosci.*, 21 May, 9: 266.

Bellis, M. A., Hardcastle, K., Ford, K., Hughes, K., Ashton, K., Quigg, Z. and Butler, N. (2017), Does continuous trusted adult support in childhood impart life-course resilience against adverse childhood experiences – a retrospective study on adult health-harming behaviours and mental well-being. *BMC Psychiatry*, 23 March, 17(1): 110.

Berne, E. (1979) *What Do You Say After You Say Hello?* New York: Bantam (original work published in 1972).

Bertrand Russell (1929) BrainyQuote.com. Available at: www.brainyquote. com/quotes/bertrand_russell_100730.

Bowlby, J. (1973) *Attachment and Loss: Volume 2 – separation, anxiety and anger*. London: Hogarth Press.

Bowlby, J. (1978) *Attachment and Loss: Volume 3 – loss, sadness and depression*. Harmondsworth: Penguin.

Bowlby, J. (1979) *The Making and Breaking of Affectional Bonds*. London: Tavistock.

Bowlby J. (1988) *A Secure Base: Clinical applications of attachment theory*. London: Routledge.

Burke Harris, N. (2015) Summit – adverse childhood experience and toxic stress. A public health crisis. The Area Health Education Center of Washington State University.

Burklund, L. J., Creswell J. D., Irwin M. R. and Lieberman, M. D. (2014) The common and distinct neural bases of affect labelling and reappraisal in healthy adults. *Front. Psychol.*, 24 March, 5: 221.

Byatt, A. S. (1997) *Still Life*. London: Scribner.

Carroll, L. (1856/2003) *Alice's Adventures in Wonderland and Through the Looking Glass*. London: Penguin Classics.

Chapman, B. P.,Fiscella, K.,Kawachi, I.,Duberstein, P. andMuennig, P. (2013) Emotion suppression and mortality risk over a 12-year follow-up. *J Psychosom Res*, October, 75(4): 381–385.

Chester, D., Eisenberger, N., Pond, R., Richman, S., Bushman, B. and DeWall, C. (2013) The interactive effect of social pain and executive functioning on aggression: An fMRI experiment. *Social Cognitive and Affective Neuroscience*, 1–6. Available at: www.ncbi.nlm.nih.gov/pmc/articles/ PMC4014110/.

Clarkson, P. (1989) *Gestalt Counselling in Action* (Counselling in Action series). London: SAGE Publications.

Coleridge, S. T. (1992) *Rime of the Ancient Mariner*. New York: Atheneum.

Craik, D. (1859) *A Life for a Life*. Montana: Kessinger Publishing.

Dickerson, S., Gruenewald, T. and Kernenv, M. (2004) When the social self is threatened: Shame, physiology, and health. *Journal of Personality*, December.

Dinnage, R. (1990) *The Ruffian on the Stair: Reflections on death*. London: Viking.

Dube, S. R., Felitti, V. J., Dong, M., Giles, W. H. and Anda, R. F. (2003) The impact of adverse childhood experiences on health problems: Evidence from four birth cohorts dating back to 1900. *Preventive Medicine* 37(3): 268–277.

Durante, D. and Dunson, B. (2016) Bayesian inference and testing of group differences in brain networks. *Bayesian Analysis*. Available at: https://projecteuclid.org/euclid.ba/1479179031.

Eisenberger, N. (2012) The pain of social disconnection: Examining the shared neural underpinnings of physical and social pain. *Nat Rev Neurosci*, 3 May, 13(6): 421–434.

Euripides (2017/431 BC) *Medea*. CreateSpace Independent Publishing Platform.

Field, T. (2017a) Prenatal anxiety effects: A review. *Infant Behav. Dev.*, November, 49: 120–128.

Field, T. (2017b) Prenatal depression risk factors, developmental effects and interventions: A review. *J. Pregnancy Child Health*, February, 4(1): 301.

Field, T., Diego, M., Hernandez-Reif, M., Salman, F., Schanberg, S., Kuhn, C., Yando, R. and Bendell, D. (2002) Prenatal anger effects on the fetus and neonate. *Journal of Obstetrics and Gynaecology* 22(3): 260–266.

Fosha, D. (2000) *The Transforming Power of Affect*. New York: Basic Books.

Freud, S. (1915) Repression, in *On Metapsychology: The theory of psychoanalysis*, vol 11. *The Penguin Freud Library*, Richards, A. and Strachey, J. (eds), Strachey J (trans), Harmondsworth: Penguin, pp. 139–157.

Gardner, W. H. (ed.) (1970) *Poems and Prose of Gerard Manley Hopkins*. Harmondsworth: Penguin.

Gerhardt, S. (2014) *Why Love Matters: How affection shapes a baby's brain*. Kings Lynn: Brunner-Routledge.

Giovacchini, P. L. (1989) *Countertransference Triumphs and Catastrophes*. Northvale, NJ: Aronson.

Goodall, J. (1990) *Through a Window: My thirty years with the chimpanzees of Gombe*. Boston, MA: Houghton, Mifflin and Company.

Gottman, J. (1993) *What Predicts Divorce?* Mahwah, NJ: Lawrence Erlbaum Associates.

Gottman, J. (1995) *Why Marriages Succeed or Fail: And how you can make yours last*. New York: Simon & Schuster.

Gottman, J. (2012) Four Negative Patterns that Predict Divorce (Parts 1 and 2). Accessed at: www.youtube.com/watch?v=FJDN3PKZ1KE; and www.youtube.com/watch?v=o5OdpPodpNY.

Gottman, J., Katz, L. and Hooven, C. (1996) Parental meta-emotion philosophy and the emotional life of families: Theoretical models and preliminary data. *Journal of Family Psychology* 10(3): 243–268.

Gough, T. (1987) *Couples Arguing*. London: Darton, Longman & Todd.

Halpern, H. (1983) *Women Who Love Too Much: How to break their addiction to a person*. New York: Bantam.

Hillman, J. (1983) *Healing Fiction*. USA: Spring Publications.

Holt-Lunstad, J., Smith, T., Baker, M., Harris, T. and Stephenson, D. (2015) Loneliness and social isolation as risk factors for mortality: A meta-analytic review. *Perspect. Psychol. Sci*, March, 10(2): 227–237.

Horney, K. (1992) *Our Inner Conflicts: A constructive theory of neurosis*. New York: W. W. Norton & Company.

Hornstein, E. A. and Eisenberger, N. I. (2017) Unpacking the buffering effect of social support figures: Social support attenuates fear acquisition. *PLoS One*, 2 May, 12(5).

Hornstein, E. A., Fanselow, M. S. and Eisenberger, N. I. (2016) A safe haven: Investigating social-support figures as prepared safety stimuli. *Psychol. Sci.*, August, 27(8):1051–1060.

Hughes, D. and Baylin J. (2012) *Brain-Based Parenting: The Neuroscience of Caregiving for Healthy Attachment*. New York: W. W. Norton & Co.

Jaremka, L., Glaser, R., Malarkey, W. and Kiecolt-Glaser, J. (2013) Marital distress prospectively predicts poorer cellular immune function. *Psychoneuroendocrinology*, November, 38(11): 2713–2719.

Johnson, K. V. A. and Dunbar, R. I. M. (2016) Pain tolerance predicts human social network size. *Scientific Reports* 6: 25267.

Johnson, S. (2004) *The Practice of Emotionally Focused Couple Therapy*. London: Brunner-Routledge.

Johnson, S. (2017) *Becoming an Emotionally Focused Couple Therapist: The workbook*. London: Routledge.

Keegan, P. (ed.) (1993) *Collected Poems of Ted Hughes*. London: Faber & Faber.

Laing, R. (1967) *The Divided Self: An existential study in sanity and madness.* London: Penguin Classics.

Lane, R. D., Ryan, L., Nadel, L. and Greenberg, L. (2015) Memory reconsolidation, emotional arousal and the process of change in psychotherapy: New insights from brain science. *Behav. Brain Sci.*, January, 38.

Lanius, R. A., Hopper, J. and Menon, R. (2003) Individual differences in a husband and wife who developed PTSD after a motor vehicle accident: A functional MR1 case study. *American Journal of Psychiatry* 160(4): 667–669.

Lewis, C. S. (1966) *A Grief Observed.* London: Faber & Faber (original work published in 1961).

Lieberman, M. D., Eisenberger, N. I., Crockett, M. J., Tom, S. M., Pfeifer, J. H. and Way, B. M. (2007) Putting feelings into words: Affect labeling disrupts amygdala activity to affective stimuli. *Psychological Science* 18: 421–428.

Lowenfeld, M. (1931) *The World Technique.* London: Allen & Unwin.

Loydell, R. (1992) *Distances.* New York: Midpoint Trade Books.

Martikainen, P. T. and Valkonen, T. (1996) Excess mortality of unemployed men and women during a period of rapidly increasing unemployment. *Lancet,* 5 October, 348(9032): 909–912.

McDougall, J. (1989) *Theatres of the Body: A psychoanalytical approach to psychosomatic illness.* London: Free Association Books.

McGinnis, S. and Jenkins, P. (2006) *Good Practice Guidance for Counselling in Schools.* Rugby: British Association for Counselling and Psychotherapy.

Miller, A. (1987) *For Your Own Good: The roots of violence in child-rearing,* Hannum, H. and H. (trans). London: Virago.

Mitchell, S. (1988) *Relational Concepts in Psychoanalysis: An integration,* 5th edn. New York: Guilford Press.

Mitchell, S. (2004) *Relationality, from Attachment to Intersubjectivity.* London: Analytic Press.

Moore, T. (1994a) *Soul Mates.* New York: Harper Perennial.

Moore, T. (1994b) *Care of the Soul.* New York: Harper.

Morelli, S. A., Torre, J. B., Eisenberger, N. I. (2014) The neural bases of feeling understood and not understood. *Soc. Cogn. Affect Neurosci.*, December, 9(12): 1890–1896.

Moriguchi, Y., Decety, J., Ohnishi, T., Maeda, M., Matsuda, H. and Komaki, G. (2007) Empathy and judging other's pain: An fMRI study of alexithymia. *Cerebral Cortex*, September, 17(9): 2223–2225.

Moyal, N., Cohen, N., Henik, A., Anholt, G. E. (2015) Emotion regulation as a main mechanism of change in psychotherapy. *Behav. Brain Sci.* 38.

Norwood, R. (1986) *Women Who Love Too Much.* London: Arrow.

Nummenmaa, L., Manninen, S., Tuominen, L., Hirvonen, J., Kalliokoski, K. K., Nuutila, P., Jääskeläinen, I. P., Hari, R., Dunbar, R. I. and Sams, M. (2015) Adult attachment style is associated with cerebral-opioid receptor availability in humans. *Hum. Brain Mapp*, September, 36(9): 3621–3628.

Orbach, S. (1994) *What's Really Going on Here.* London: Virago.

Panksepp, J. (2001) The Long-term psychobiological consequences of infant emotions prescriptions for the twenty-first century. *Neuro-Psychoanalysis* 3: 149–178.

Panksepp, J. (2002) Private communication.

Panksepp, J. (2003) Affective consciousness and the origins of human mind: A critical role of brain research on animal emotions. *Impulse* 57: 47–60.

Panksepp, J. and Biven, L. (2012) *The Archaeology of Mind: Neuroevolutionary origins of human emotion.* New York: W. W. Norton & Co.

Peele, S. and Brodsky, A. (1976) *Love and Addiction.* New York: Signet.

Pennebaker, J. W. (1993) Putting stress into words: Health, linguistic, and therapeutic implications. *Behavioural Research Therapy* 31(6): 539–548.

Pennebaker, J. W. (1995) Emotion, disclosure and health: An overview, in Pennebaker, J. W. (ed.) *Emotion, Disclosure, and Health,* Washington, DC: American Psychological Association, pp. 3–10.

Pennebaker, J. W. and Chung, C. K. (2011) Expressive writing: Connections to physical and mental health, in Friedman, in H. S. (ed.) *The Oxford Handbook of Health Psychology.* New York, NY: Oxford University Press, pp. 417–437.

Perls, F. (1969) *Gestalt Therapy Verbatim.* Highland, NY: Gestalt Journal Press.

Perry, B. (2002) Childhood experience and the expression of genetic potential: What childhood neglect tells us about nature and nurture. *Brain and Mind* 3: 79.

Polster, E. and Polster, M. (1973) *Gestalt Therapy Integrated.* New York: Brunner/Mazel.

Polster, E. (1987) *Every Person's Life is Worth a Novel*. New York: Norton.

Remarque, E. M. (1929) *All Quiet on the Western Front*. Boston: Little, Brown.

Resnick, M. (1998) Technologies for lifelong kindergarten. *Educational Technology Research and Development* 46(4): 43–55.

Resnick, R. (1993) Personal communication during couples therapy training at the Metanoia Trust, London.

Ricks, C. (ed.) (1999) *The Oxford Book of English Verse*. Oxford: OUP.

Schoenewolf, G. (1991) *The Art of Hating*. Northvale, NJ: Jason Aronson.

Schore, A. (2003) *Affect Dysregulation and Disorders of the Self*. New York: Norton.

Schore, A. N. (1994) *Affect Regulation and the Origins of the Self – The Neurobiology of Emotional Development*. Mahwah, NJ: Lawrence Erlbaum Associates.

Seeman, T. E. (2014) Health promoting effects of friends and family on health outcomes in older adults. *Am. J. Health Promot.*, July – August, 14(6): 362–370.

Segal, J. (1985) *Phantasy in Everyday Life: A psychoanalytical approach to understanding ourselves*. Harmondsworth: Penguin.

Siegel, D. (1999) *The Developing Mind*. New York: Guilford Press.

Sroufe, A., Collins, A., Carlson, E. and Egeland, B. (2005) *The Development of the Person*. New York: Guilford Press.

Stern, D. (1990) *Diary of a Baby: What your child sees, feels, and experiences*. New York: Basic Books.

Storr, A. (1972) *The Dynamics of Creation*, 1st edn. Scribner.

Sullivan, H. (1986) *The Interpersonal Theory of Psychiatry*. New York: Norton.

Sunderland M. (1993) *Draw on Your Emotions*. Milton Keynes: Speechmark.

Sunderland, M. (2002) *Using Storytelling as a Therapeutic Tool with Children*. Milton Keynes: Speechmark.

Sunderland, M. (2010) *Monica Plum's Horrid Problem: A story for children of troubled parents*. London: Routledge.

Sunderland, M. (2016) *What Every Parent Needs to Know*. London: Dorling Kindersley.

Sunderland, M. and Armstrong, N. (2018) *Draw on Your Emotions: A practical workbook for emotional literacy*. London: Routledge.

Teo, A. (2015) Does mode of contact with different types of social relationships predict depression among older adults? Evidence from a nationally representative survey. *Journal of the American Geriatrics Society*, October.

Tessina, T. B. and Smith, R. K. (1980) *How to Be a Couple and Still be Free*. Newcastle, CA: Newcastle Publishing Co.

Trachtenberg, P. (1988) *The Casanova Complex: Compulsive lovers and their women*. New York: Poseidon.

Uvnas-Moberg, K. (2011) *The Oxytocin Factor: Tapping the hormone of calm, love and healing*. Cambridge, MA: Da Capo Press.

Uvnas-Moberg, K. and Petersson M. (2005) Oxytocin, a mediator of anti-stress, well-being, social interaction, growth and healing. *Z. Psychosom. Med. Psychother*. 51(1): 57–80.

Van der Kolk, B. (2015) *The Body Keeps the Score*. New York: Penguin Random House.

Winnicott, D. W. (1964) Review of memories, dreams, reflections by CJ Jung. *International Journal of Psychoanalysis* 45: 450–455.

Winterson, J. (1995) *Art and Lies*. London: Vintage.

Yalom, I. (1980) *Existential Psychotherapy*. New York: Basic Books.

Ybarra, O., Burnstein, E., Winkielman, P., Keller, M. C., Manis, M., Chan, E. and Rodriguez, J. (2008) Mental exercising through simple socializing: Social interaction promotes general cognitive functioning.Pers. Soc. Psychol. Bull., February, 34(2): 248–259.

Zinker, J. (1978) *Creative Process in Gestalt Therapy*. New York: Vintage.

Images used

'Conflict between father and defiant teenage daughter'. Alamy Stock Photo. Available at: www.alamy.com/stock-photo-conflict-between-father-and-defiant-teenage-daughter-174300095.html.

'Dialogue between woman and man'. Alamy Stock Photo. Available at: www.alamy.com/stock-photo-dialogue-between-woman-and-man-169892507.html.